MORE WORDS YOU NEED

Teacher's Book and Answer Key

by B Rudzka, J Channell, Y Putseys, P Ostyn

MACMILLAN
PUBLISHERS

First published 1985
Reprinted 1986, 1988, 1990

Published by *Macmillan Publishers Ltd*
London and Basingstoke

ISBN 0–333–37510–6

Printed in Hong Kong

More words you need.
   Teacher's book.
    1. Vocabulary———Problems, exercises, etc.
    2. English language———Text-books for foreigners
    I. Rudzka, B.
    428.1'076   PE1128

    ISBN 0–333–37510–6

Contents

Preface   iv

Introduction   1
  1 Who is *More Words You Need* for?   1
  2 What should the student already know?   1
  3 Which words are presented?   1
  4 What variety of English does this book teach?   1
  5 Why focus on vocabulary?   2

Linguistic theory and the language learner   4
  1 Semantic field theory   4
  2 Psychological validity   4
  3 Componential analysis   5
  4 Collocation   5

Organisation of the Student's Book   6
  1 Texts   6
  2 Glosses   6
  3 Discussion   7
  4 Word Study   7
  5 Exercises   7

Suggestions for using the book   9
  1 The texts and topics for discussion   9
  2 The word study sections   10
  3 The exercises   11
  4 Class time   12

Words posing pronunciation problems, listed by unit and text   13

Key to the exercises   15

References and selected further reading   57

Preface

More Words You Need, like its companion *The Words You Need,* sets out to organise the acquisition of language skills within the context of a structured approach to vocabulary teaching and learning. The approach used is a completely new one, adapting insights from theoretical linguistics and psycholinguistics to the service of the language learner.

In this teacher's book, which accompanies *More Words You Need (The Words You Need* has its own teacher's book and key), we try to answer the sort of questions teachers will want to ask. We explain the teaching methods used, and give practical guidance on the many and varied uses to which the material can be put. In order to make full use of this new material, the teacher may need some knowledge of the linguistic and pedagogic theories behind it. To this end, a brief introduction has also been included. We stress to those hard-pressed teachers who often turn past such pages to the practical ones, that *it is really essential for them to read this short theoretical section.*

Finally, we would like to add that there is no one right way to use this book. Our guidelines are meant only as suggestions, and the teacher has freedom to exploit the material in any way he pleases. We hope it will prove both enjoyable and worthwhile.

B Rudzka, J Channell, Y Putseys, P Ostyn

Introduction

1 Who is *More Words You Need* for?

This book is for post-intermediate and advanced students of English either as a foreign or as a second language. By post-intermediate and advanced we mean for example:
   post-secondary students of English (ie those in Universities and Colleges)
   students preparing for advanced academic study using English medium
   trainee teachers of English at all levels
   summer school students
   students studying for Cambridge Proficiency or similar level exams
   translators and interpreters
   and generally any student who has reached the stage of adequate communication, and wants to push his English towards a working equivalent of native speaker English.

2 What should the student already know?

a   The basic grammatical structures of English. There is no explicit grammar teaching in this book, although a wealth of grammatically interesting material affords the teacher the opportunity to teach advanced grammar points from it, if he wishes.
b   A vocabulary of about 3,000 basic and frequent English words.
   This book is a little more advanced than its companion volume *The Words You Need,* but it is not necessary to have studied *The Words You Need* before using this book.

3 Which words are presented?

The vocabulary taught covers a wide range of subjects and is designed to improve the student's general level of communication, by giving him more words he can use.
For instance, he knows the word *begin,* and we add *commence, initiate, instigate* and *launch.* We have excluded very unusual words, and those having limited specialist uses.

4 What variety of English does the book teach?

English is spoken as a first language in many parts of the world and exists in many different varieties. It is also in wide use as a second and foreign language. It is obvious that Britain no longer has exclusive rights over dictating what is acceptable 'right' English. Nevertheless British English is widely accepted as an ideal standard towards which learners are guided. For this reason we have placed our emphasis on *standard British English.*

However, given the large volume of published material written in American English, which the student at this level cannot fail to meet, we have deliberately selected texts from both British and American sources. In marking the differences between American and British English we do not expect the student to master both varieties or be able to 'translate' from one to the other. What we do think necessary is for him to be able to understand both, and recognize the differences between them. The same is true for any non-standard English which occurs in some of our more colloquial texts.

For American English (referred to as *Am*) we have adopted the following system: all British spellings which are different from American spellings are listed on page iii of the Student's Book, and are not noted in individual texts. Differences of vocabulary and syntax are explained in the glosses. Since our emphasis is on British English (referred to as *Br*), we provide *Br* equivalents of *Am* expressions and words, but do not translate *Br* expressions into *Am*.

5 Why focus on vocabulary?

When a student has mastered the basic grammatical structures of English, he might well have a basic vocabulary of 1,500-2,500 words. What he needs to acquire at this stage is more words, words to put into the structures he knows. Usually he is told to 'go away and read as much as possible', the hope being that in some magic way exposure to large numbers of words will suddenly lead to rapid vocabulary extension. In this way, the student will probably learn to recognize new words, but is this sufficient? Let's look at some typical lexical errors which students make and with which all teachers are familiar.

The first type of error happens when the student has an idea of the basic sense of the words, but does not know:

a   which other words it will combine with (its *collocational properties*), or
b   how it relates to other words of similar meaning.

Here are a few examples:
*to put up a campaign
*she laughed broadly
*a good-looking view
*to estimate the evidence
(We follow the usual practice of marking an unacceptable expression or sentence with an *.)

Another common tendency among students is to overuse a limited set of words whose sense and collocational properties they are sure of. This results in a flat, uninteresting style and failure to express the variety of ideas they want to communicate, as in:

a good teacher/lesson/meal/day/girl/university

The third type of error arises from the student's erroneous (but natural) assumption that the collocational properties of a new word he has just met are the same as its translation equivalent in his own language. Here, his native language semantic competence interferes with his English performance. For example, French speakers make the following errors:

*He closed the door with the key. (locked)
*a voyage by train. (journey)
*I made an experience in the laboratory. (experiment)
*When could I touch Mr Ostyn? (contact)

2

and Dutch speakers:

*You can easily overlook the several possibilities with their own value. (look at .
. . at the same time)
*I sacked in mathematics. (failed)

When a student meets a new word either in a text or in conversation, he can usually only learn that it is correct in that context. If he looks it up in a dictionary he will find a definition, and perhaps some examples, but this won't help him much when he wants to know if it will be suitable in another context, nor will it help him to know how it relates to other words with similar meaning.

There are two things, besides basic sense, which a student needs to know about every new word he wants to make part of his active competence:

a   How does it relate to other words with similar meaning?
b   Which other words can it be used with, and in which contexts?

Linguistic theory and the language learner

Linguistics tries to provide a description of all the sentences of a language under investigation, which reflects the intuitions of its native speakers about when and how those sentences should be used. While the language learner is not, of course, consciously interested in 'providing a description' of the language he is learning, it is obvious that he must in some sense acquire all the information which would enable him to do so, since it is this same information which enables him to speak the language correctly. Given this similarity between the goals of the linguist, and those of the language learner, it is not surprising that some of the linguist's ways of investigating language are useful to the learner.

1 Semantic field theory

Particularly relevant to vocabulary acquisition is semantic field theory. This theory departs from the premise that the vocabulary of a language, far from being a random collection of words, consists of interrelating networks, made up of sets of semantically similar words. An example of a semantic field is the set of 'kinship terms': **mother, father, son, daughter, brother, sister, aunt, uncle,** etc. Clearly these words share some aspect of meaning which is not present, say, in the item **cloud.** Another example of a field would be 'verbs of movement': **walk, run, stroll, amble, trot, jog.** But this field differs from kinship terms in the sense that here we may want to say that **stroll** is also part of another field consisting of **wander, stroll, roam, ramble.** Equally, **run** is a member of the field 'moving fast': **run, sprint, canter, gallop, dash.** It would be possible to go on assembling fields until we had covered the whole vocabulary of English, and we would want to place many words in perhaps two or three different fields. It is in this sense that vocabulary should be seen as a set of interrelating networks. By deploying this approach in teaching, we have at our disposal a systematic framework within which to present words to the learner.

2 Psychological validity

In addition to the practicality of this approach, there is evidence to show that the mind makes use of semantic similarity in finding words from memory for use in speech. Studies of slips of the tongue (ie when a speaker produces a wrong word, realises it, and corrects himself) made by native speakers of English have shown that many wrong words, far from being random mistakes, actually share some aspect of meaning with the intended word, for example:
I have my book and my **jigsaw** . . . I mean **crossword**
We **invited** him to . . . **asked** him to buy crisps
I really **like** to . . . **hate** to get up in the morning

4

Sometimes the 'wrong' word is a mixture of two words from the same semantic field:

I swindged (switched/changed)
momentaneous (instantaneous/momentary)
herrible (terrible/horrible) (Fromkin, 1973)

A second type of evidence comes from the speech of people with certain kinds of brain damage. In tests of reading, some of them, instead of saying the word they are shown, consistently say another word from the same semantic field, for example **canary** read as **parrot, ill** as **sick, city** as **town** and **bush** as **tree**. (Marshall and Newcombe, 1966.)

This evidence suggests that the mind takes account of meaning in the way it stores and retrieves words. It may be that the mind stores words in the kind of semantic sets described above. If this is the case, it is clear that we should teach words in semantic fields in order to help students to remember them.

3 Componential analysis

Words belong to the same semantic field when they share some aspects of meaning but few words share all aspects. Synonymy is often a confusing rather than helpful notion to the student, since there are so few English words which are interchangeable in all contexts. For example, **run** and **sprint** are similar in both being verbs which express fast movement by human beings, but they differ in that **sprint** is used for a faster movement, over a short distance. Linguists describe such differences and similarities by breaking down the meaning of words into different pieces known as *semantic features*[1] (sometimes 'components', but we shall use 'features' throughout). For **run** and **sprint** this might be:

run: [+ move] [+ by feet] [+ quickly] [+ on land] [+ placing down one foot after another]
sprint: [+ move] [+ by feet] [+ as quickly as possible] [+ on land] [+ placing down one foot after another] [+ over a short distance]

Each feature is enclosed in a pair of square brackets. Note that they share some, but not all, features. This clear representation of differences and similarities between two words is exactly what the student learning new vocabulary needs.

4 Collocation

One of the main difficulties students encounter in relation to new items of vocabulary is knowing what their collocational properties are (which words they will go with), apart from the one collocation in which they have met the word. The most extreme version of collocational theory says that the meaning of a

[1] Note that our presentation of semantic features departs considerably from that adopted by the specialist in semantics. Being interested in analysing the meaning of words, and not in teaching them, the semanticist employs one-word feature specifications. For teaching purposes, however, such specifications are not always suitable. The student is not likely to grasp the meaning of a word on the basis of a mere inventory of one-word features. It appears that at least some of the links between the features must be expressed verbally, and instead of one-word specifications we have often used whole phrases to elucidate areas of meaning.

Another departure from the usual practice of semanticists was to include in some of our semantic analyses information about syntactic constraints and the non-linguistic context in which words can be used.

word is only accessible through its collocations. It is clear that for the student of English, an important aspect of knowing a word is knowing its collocational properties.

Language in use is very flexible, and the collocational possibilities of any word do not form a fixed set. That is to say, while English speakers agree on more typical collocations, there are many other collocations which some people would use, and others not, not to mention metaphorical and creative uses of language, which result in quite new collocations constantly being formed. A set of collocations is not therefore a list of all the ways in which a word can be used, but rather a set of examples of how a word is usually used. For the student, collocations are points of reference for him to use in forming his own collocations.

Used together, semantic field theory, componential analysis and the collocational approach give us a systematic, clear and precise way of presenting the vocabulary of English to students.

Organization of the Student's Book

More Words You Need is made up of ten units each built around a different theme. Each unit consists of:
Texts
Glosses
Discussion Questions
Word Study
Exercises

1 Texts

The texts selected are all authentic. We have found that advanced students feel that specially written material in some sense talks down to them, and is not 'real' English. They far prefer authentic texts, even if they are a little more difficult.

Our selection covers a wide range of topics relevant not only in Britain and the USA but worldwide, such as crime and punishment, health, eating and drinking, and the changing role of women.

The texts are intended to serve a double purpose: to present students with challenging ideas and to provide a natural context of correct spoken and written English in which words can be learned.

2 Glosses

The selection of words for the glosses which accompany each text is based on our teaching experience with advanced students of different linguistic backgrounds, and given their varying requirements, we preferred to gloss too many words rather than too few. Therefore not all the glosses will be useful to all students. As an important aspect of vocabulary acquisition is learning to guess the meaning of unknown words from their context, we have not glossed those words whose sense is deduceable from the text. If necessary the student may, of course, check the accuracy of his 'guess' in a dictionary. In fact, we hope to encourage students to use monolingual dictionaries, and therefore our glosses are rather more indications of which meaning in the dictionary is the relevant one, than full definitions of the words concerned.

We do not, however, preclude the use of a bilingual dictionary for finding the names of birds, animals and plants, since we found that glossing these involved unnecessarily complicated, and not always very helpful, definitions.

3 Discussion

Our suggestions for discussion are not only an invitation to exchange ideas but also a pretext for using the words studied. Only when the student can use the words correctly and in a spontaneous way will the aim of the book have been fulfilled.

4 Word Study

Words are taught in semantic fields, or in contrastive pairs consisting of two members of a field. We single out words from our texts and add other words to make up a field. The semantic fields in any unit result directly from the vocabulary in the texts. This means that no field is introduced unless at least one of its members is illustrated in the texts of the unit in question. The remaining members of a given field are often drawn from texts presented in other units. This way of introducing words resembles the natural way a student would meet new vocabulary, experiencing it in situations, but has the added advantage of systematic explanation.

The first Word Study in the Student's Book contains detailed explanation and guidance notes. These are intended to help teachers to present the Word Study analyses to their students. It is not necessary for students to understand the theoretical (linguistic) background in order to understand the Word Study. However you will find that some groups of students will benefit from some theoretical explanation. Once the students have worked through the Word Study of Unit 1 with the teacher, they will be able to study the Word Study in other units on their own, referring back if necessary to the guidance notes in Unit 1.

5 Exercises

An important aspect of learning new words is the opportunity to practise them. Our emphasis is on systematic repetition of words by means of different types of exercises. Each unit (except Unit 1) contains two sorts of exercises:

   a   exercises which practise the words and expressions used in the texts and Word Study of the unit

   b   revision exercises which offer further practice of words from preceding units.

The student is now aware of the concepts of field theory, componential analysis and collocation, so his knowledge of the meaning and collocations of particular words is reinforced by exercises specially designed to reflect these concepts. Examples of these are:

1 What are the similarities and differences between the following pairs?
1 to see sth/to look at sth   2 to surprise/to astonish   3 to pour tea/to spill tea
4 an ability/a skill   5 paint/varnish   6 a target/a goal

This exercise requires the student to make an informal feature analysis of the words in each pair.

2 Choose from the words in brackets the one which best fits the given context.
1 In London you see tramps . . . the street, looking for something and looking for nothing. **(roam, walk, go)**

2 As we reached the top of the hill a . . . view stretched out before us. **(good-looking, handsome, beautiful)**

This tests collocational competence, and also the student's knowledge of how words in a field relate to each other.

3 What can you . . .?
1 be fed up with   2 be horrified by   3 overlook   4 discriminate against

This tests collocational competence.
In addition, there are exercises designed to expand the student's awareness of the interaction of linguistic and contextual factors, eg

4 Consider the following words and give as many contextual details as you can.
1 to trudge   2 to amend   3 to smack   4 to intercept   5 to mature   6 stereotype

Other exercises invite the student to reflect on the figurative use or on the stylistic properties of words.
There are exercises asking for summaries of texts including specific words, for definitions of words, and for creative writing following the style and vocabulary of example texts.
We also have continuous pieces of prose in which the students must fit logical and contextually suitable words from a given list. This encourages sensitivity to context. Finally, crosswords provide a more relaxing practice of the words learnt.
All these exercises aim specifically at helping the student to avoid the kind of lack of precision and over-generalization which so often characterizes his speech.

Suggestions for using the book

1 The texts and topics for discussion

The texts presented in our book vary considerably in form and content and as such lend themselves to a wide variety of uses. At the outset, we would like to dissuade you from following a practice which is still quite common among teachers, at least in our part of the world. What we have in mind is the practice of reading aloud each text in class. Your time is far too precious to be spent on activities which the student can effectively carry out on his own. We suggest, however, that you teach the words posing pronunciation problems. You will find them listed in the section of the book that follows this one.

When asking the students to prepare the texts, point out to them that they will remember the words better if the texts are re-read at one or two day intervals. Whereas they need to go over *all* the texts, you may well prefer to devote class time to the close study of one or two in particular.

There are many ways of handling a text and you should try to vary your approach from lesson to lesson. Here are a few suggestions. In addition to the well-known practice of you or the students asking questions on the texts or the students summarizing the texts, you could get them to concentrate on the style or kind of English used. For example, you could conduct a search for the main characteristics of American English in texts such as 'The Pygmalion Effect Lives' (Unit 1), 'Art Yarrington's Marathon' (6), 'The New Housewife Blues' (7) or 'Solar Energy' (10). Articles from *The Sunday Post, Weekend* and *The Daily Mirror* can be used to develop the student's sensitivity to colloquial English, for example, 'Carry on Fidgeting' (6), 'Believe this and you'll believe anything' (7), and 'The experts have done it again' (9). By contrast, formal written English is illustrated in texts such as 'Responses after observation of movie violence' (4), 'Standard, non-standard or both?' (5), 'Vandalism and violence in school and society' (8), or 'Underground architecture' (10).

Another activity for which the texts may serve as a springboard is role playing. Depending on the subject matter, you divide the class into pairs, assigning the roles of journalist and scientist, doctor and resuscitated patient, lawyer and client, interviewer and marathon runner, and so on. For the sake of variety, you assign a third student the role of a reporter who listens in on the conversation between the other two and summarizes what was said, or, a good exercise for prospective teachers, makes a note of mistakes.

Many of the texts can also be used as a starting point for discussion. Like role playing, discussions are most effective when carried out in small groups. Therefore, we strongly recommend that you divide the class into groups of 3-4 students, ensuring that there is a good student in each group to guide the conversation. As students often do not know how to start a discussion, they may want to use our lists of topics. If, however, they feel inspired, they should follow their own line of interest. The important thing is that they engage in a spontaneous exchange of ideas. In order not to stifle spontaneity or inhibit the more timid, we suggest that you do not correct their mistakes immediately. (You may take notes and comment on them at the end of the lesson). It is imperative, however, that you show your interest in what they are doing by supplying unknown words, introducing new ideas or stimulating the discussion by making controversial statements. Each of the groups may, of course, talk about something different. In fact, we often divide our students according to what they want to discuss. They obviously feel more at ease with topics of their own choice. Incidentally, we have found out that they express themselves more effectively and derive greater enjoyment from the discussion when they prepare the topics in advance. This preparation usually involves a close reading of our lists of suggestions for discussion and grouping words relevant to a given topic. Some students are very keen on jotting down beforehand what they intend to say.

From time to time the whole class may wish to have a discussion. One way of organizing such a general discussion is to let students take turns in asking and answering questions or in reporting on personal experience. Our own students had a very successful discussion session of this kind on the texts about discrimination against women.

Whichever of the activities suggested you choose, bear in mind that variety is the best way of maintaining the students' interest. It may therefore be advisable to spend no more than 20-30 minutes on activities revolving around the texts, unless the students become engaged in a very lively discussion.

2 The Word Study

Here are some activities which can be used first to introduce, and then later to exploit, the notions of semantic field, collocational grid and scale.

a Semantic fields
One way to introduce the idea of semantic fields is the following:
Study the text 'Aye he's a changed man' (Unit 1). Draw the students' attention to the colloquial expression *to fetch sb a clout.* Refer to the word *hit* (which they probably know). Starting with the word *hit,* ask them to think of, or find from a dictionary, words which describe similarly the action of one person hitting another. Put the list of words on the board. (You may have to provide some of them yourself.)

Next, discuss with the class the similarities and differences between the words. What is the difference between *smack* and *clout?* Are *slap* and *smack* the same? In this way the students will make (orally) an informal feature analysis. Ask them to think up example sentences for each verb.

Finally, ask them to look at Grid 7 in the Word Study, and show them how it sets out visually the sort of points they have just been making orally. Explain the collocational grid (you will need to explain the word *collocate*) and show how it could be expanded to include any additional examples they may have made.

Another activity is to ask each student to assemble a semantic field. The first time they do this you can give 'starter' words, and ask them to prepare to describe the words in their field in class. In small group or pairwork, each person describes their field and others discuss and make suggestions. Finally each group chooses its best semantic field to present to the class. This activity is a very good indicator of which students have, and which have not, grasped the concept of semantic fields.

While commenting on the grids, make use of the special instructions on Unit 1 printed on pages 7-15 of the Student's Book. It will often happen that you need to draw the students' attention to the syntactic and stylistic properties of words in a given field.

b Collocational grids
It is important that students understand that the collocations given are not the only correct ones in any absolute sense. Most native speakers would accept the collocations given, many would accept others which we do not give. A very useful activity which enables students to discover at first hand the variability of collocation, is the following. Provide each student with a blank version of any of our collocational grids. Ask them to question two or three native speakers as to which collocations are acceptable. They will come back with a great variety of interesting and useful information about the words involved, and they will find complete agreement about some collocations and almost none about others.

Note: where native speakers are not available, very advanced non-natives can be asked. Dictionaries will also provide some examples.

c Scales
As with the collocational grids, students need to realise that the information given in scales is not exact. Encourage them to do their own 'research' on the relationships within groups of words, by asking native speakers and looking at dictionaries and texts.

Once your students become familiar with the mechanism of analysing words into smaller units of meaning, we suggest that you do not discuss every single part of the word study in class. Ask the students to read the section at home and mark anything that is not quite clear to them. When you next meet, go over the points that caused problems and encourage the students to go back to the word study each time they encounter a difficulty in an exercise. Encourage them also to re-read in a systematic fashion the example sentences which accompany the grids. This will enable them not only to master the meaning of the words illustrated but also to grasp the situations in which they can be used.

3 The exercises

After the students have worked their way through the texts and the word study, they can start on the exercises. Once more, the number of exercises covered in class will largely depend on the type of student you are working with and the time allotted. In any case, we suggest that your students prepare the exercises beforehand. In view of the considerable time this will require, they should not be expected to prepare both the new and revision exercises for the same lesson.

You will have noticed that some of our exercises call for filling in all sorts of grids or finding words that fit a given definition. When going over them in class, allow only short answer periods. The student should be able to give an immediate answer; if he hesitates, then he does not know the words concerned and should be asked to study them again. He can do this easily by referring to the relevant gloss, grid or synonymous pair. Note that we do *not* expect the student to know everything that is in the grids by heart. Rather, we expect him to consult the grids as often as possible, and we use some of the more mechanical fill-in exercises as a pretext to oblige him to do so.

In addition to giving vocabulary practice, the exercises mentioned can be fun, particularly when done orally and at high speed. You can even have a game in which the students compete in two groups for the best and quickest answers.

The exercises that require more reflection and allow for variation in responses, for example 1.4, 1.9 and 1.16, are especially suitable for small group and pair work. The students can compare and evaluate each other's answers and justify the choice of synonyms, semantic features, descriptive details, etc. The need to justify one's choice is especially felt when students are asked to fill in blanks in continuous pieces of prose, to complete sentences with synonymous expressions or to describe the situation in which a given word can or must be used. While helping the students to retain the words, all these group exercises afford practice in self-expression and precision. Obviously, certain students will need this kind of practice more than others, and you could provide it at the cost of some of the easier exercises. Feel free to omit whatever you consider less useful or relevant to your students. It may be of interest to you to learn that in the case of some Dutch speaking students our derivational exercises turned out to be less important and could be dropped altogether, yet according to reports from the University of Trier, they posed a serious problem for German speaking students.

In order to let the students practise new words in written form, we have included a few exercises requiring summaries of texts or creative writing. Many of our discussion topics can also be used for written assignments.

Some of the written exercises could be tackled in class. They can be quite effective when combined with conversation. On the other hand, the time needed for written completion exercises will be spent more effectively if students do them at home and concentrate in class on comparing and justifying their answers.

All the techniques mentioned above hold for the new as well as the revision exercises. The revision exercises can, moreover, be conveniently used as informal tests. These tests might consist of only a few items, yet when administered frequently and unexpectedly, they will certainly stimulate the students to work systematically. The students could be told that there is no point in constantly covering new material if little of it is being retained, and that the idea of the test is to help them to see how much of the earlier material they still know and to refresh their memories.

4 Class time

It will be clear by now that the material of each unit is readily adaptable to class periods of varying duration and can be broken up and tackled on different days.

Assuming you are at Unit 3, you may do in class selected revision exercises from Unit 2, then organise a 20-30 minute discussion or role playing or question-and-answer period around the texts of Unit 3. The last 15 minutes could be spent on problems from the word study section of Unit 3. If you teach 90-minute periods, you will still have time for some new exercises from Unit 3.

An alternative approach would be to start with a few revision exercises from Unit 2, then pass on to the word study of Unit 3, backtrack to the texts of Unit 3, and finish with a discussion on the topics accompanying them. If you do not have the time to do the new exercises of Unit 3, you can do them at the beginning of the next lesson, before you start work on the texts or the word study of Unit 4.

We would like to stress once more that what this teachers' guide offers is only suggestions. You will undoubtedly find your own way of using the book to its best advantage.

Words posing pronunciation problems, listed by unit and text

Unit 1
Pygmalion effect Galatea, ivory, prophesy, dumb, Lenore Jacobson, IQ-test
A-level disillusionment unsuited
Night school Greenwich, sociology, knitting
A changed man locusts, clean-limbed, sterling, scathing, karate, weird, viability, Enoch
College rags blatant, dour, thesaurus

Unit 2
TV hot stuff ingredients, breakthrough, euphoria, fiber, laser, virtuosity, facsimile, via, athletic, archive, repository, crucial
No Place to Hide Senate, circuits, microwave, analysts, ahead, feasible, machines, figured out, satellite
The computer and privacy phenomenal, access, emerge, procedure, amend, inaccurate, reliable, IBM
Freedom of thought inhibit, exclusively, questionable, indigestion, stereotypes, comfortable
What's happening? violated, ethics, prohibit, vehicle, libel, disclosure

Unit 3
Cultural concepts accuracy, civilization, antiquity, events, magnitude, Taoism, infinite, estimate, linearity (linear), egotism, hustling, quantitative, transient, intuitive, pervasive, cycles, anarchy, schedule, ancestors, abiding
Every day a gift alleged, epidemic, baptismal record, arithmetic, Crimean, thread, Caucasus, figures, longevity, extensive, privileged, continuity, poultry, literate
Retirees may overburden psychiatrist, valuable, incentives, eligible
Senior power racism, demon, dawning on, mobile

Unit 4
Curb that filth articulate, interference, hitherto, homosexual, conscience, prohibited, pornography, libertarians, irreparable
Movie violence heighten, aggressively, processes, target, subsided, measurement, reinforced, injury
Book banners subversive, vernacular, wrath, Gulliver
Frightening catalogue tenement flat, wrecked, bomb hoax, Heathrow
Silent too long bawl, hypocritical, indictable, cushioned, spiritually, measured

Unit 5
Mr Whatshisname wily, browsing, bowl sb over, dreaded, rehearsed, hostile, amnesia, suing (sb for slander)
Language and sex-discrimination expertise, feminine, designated, dichotomizing, crevices, innovative, hysterical

13

Standard, non-standard   alienation, adolescent, legitimate, variety, dialect, adequate, bidialectalism
Personal space   psychiatrist, breath, inviolate, shoving, exhibited, intimate, disparate
Body language   posture, luscious, Mediterranean, flaunt, subtly

Unit 6
Exercise for ever   pursuit, dieting, sedentary, lethargic, antidote
Morbid society   epidemic, iatrogenesis, antibiotics, goads
Art Yarrington   ruggedly, diagnosis, myocardial ischemia, ECG, averaging, snarled, angiogram, catheter, inflammatory carditis
Spurious sedative   spurious, sedative
Stress the spice of life   Montreal
Fidgeting   elaborate routine, anxiety, tranquillisers
Easing a baby's way   massaged, Michael, psychosomatic
Drug hoarding   thalidomide, strychnine

Unit 7
The new housewife   Illinois, thoroughly, patronized, cumulative, resource, Massachusetts, Minneapolis, ethic, damaging, panacea, affectionate, desacralized
Drive for success   competitive, weight, alibi
Believe this   recipe, endearment, chauvinist
Women farmers   dawn, mechanization, homesteads, Iowa
A new frock   onslaught, amiable, determine, jealous, gears, swear, compromise

Unit 8
Crime and punishment   solicitor, deter, judiciary, rehabilitate, disparate, idiosyncratic, discretion, alienated
Vandalism and violence   prevalence, perennial, juvenile, estimate
Guns blaze   lethal
A Thief   scrawled, associate, gesture
Champion shoplifter   jewel(le)ry, pearl necklace
Tough guys fled   Buchanan, Karate
Cashless society   ingenious, unwary

Unit 9
The food you eat   degenerative, bologna, scrawny, diet, analyses, protein
Hounded out   growl, oven, wolfed down, breakages
Junk Food   glutamate, migraines
The experts   anxieties, caffeine, sweat
Baffling   tangerines
Austrians   obesity, breath
Spring salad   lettuce, coarsely, olives, Parmesan

Unit 10
Nightmare   nuclear fission, gasoline, sacrifice, leisure, fossil
Solar energy   legendary, hydroelectric, alternative, Connecticut, prohibitive, ultimate, orbiting, satellites
Underground architecture   architectural, catacombs, Montreal, allay
First tree   fragrance, balsam

Key to the exercises

UNIT 1

1 1 hindrance 2 awareness 3 adornment 4 enrollment 5 bloomer
6 certificate 7 accuracy 8 owner 9 fluency 10 prophecy
11 comprehension 12 pressure

2 1 a child who has lost one or both of its parents by death 2 a person
who goes on foot 3 a sculpture is a three-dimensional work of art, cut
out of stone, wood, etc 4 in an experiment a group used as a
standard for comparing and testing truth or correctness 5 a complex
network of paths through which it is difficult to find one's way
6 a statement which is accepted as true without proof 7 information
coming back to the originator about the results of an event, new
product, new process, etc 8 attract or entice, tempt (with a promise of
pleasure, etc) 9 meet by accident 10 calling or inviting to fight, to
run a race, to play a game, etc 11 filling with fury or rage
12 bringing satisfaction 13 filling with amazement, astonishing greatly
14 a sudden, violent change, eg a flood, an earthquake, a great war
15 almost the same as, very near 16 obvious, with no attempt to hide

3 1 piling into 2 signed up 3 trudging 4 budge 5 fondled
6 climate 7 rate

4 1 retort, reply, look, report, comment, review 2 the outer leaves of a
lettuce, half the texts in the book, one's youthful idealism
3 a holiday, a stay in England, good advice, good teaching
4 one's status, one's reputation, one's chances of success 5 sb's
death, a business association, a meeting 6 somebody, sb's stupidity,
sb's kindness, sb's presence, sb's skills 7 somebody, a problem, a
difficult situation 8 feelings of sympathy, awareness, enjoyment,
efforts

5 1 see Student's Book, grid A2, p 9 2 see Student's Book, grid B8, p 17

6 1 frantically 2 lure 3 evolve 4 strain 5 hustled 6 fondled
7 budge 8 recalcitrant 9 deprived 10 disguise

7 1 similar feelings about future events
different **desire** is wanting sth to happen; **expectation** is the feeling
that sth will probably happen
2 similar attitude towards certain opinions or points of view
different **creed** is a system of beliefs held by a group of people;
belief may refer to a group attitude or to a personal one
3 similar stages in production process in factories, information
processing, etc
different **input** is what you put in, and at what speed; **output** is what
is produced and at what speed

15

4 similar   both refer to good qualities
  different   **bright** refers to quickness of mind, **pretty** to physical charm
5 similar   kinds of psychological tests
  different   **a verbal test** uses words; **a non-verbal test** uses no words at all
6 similar   terms used to describe socio-economic groupings in western
            societies
  different   **a social class** is one group of people in a society who have
              similar incomes, jobs, and life styles; **the middle class** is
              the social group that is between those who are rich and
              those who are poor
7 similar   good mental attributes
  different   **wisdom** is the ability to make sound judgements about
              events and situations; **intelligence** is efficient mental ability
8 similar   rapid movement
  different   **run** is move by means of the legs; **rush** is move more
              rapidly than normal, usually for a specific reason
9 similar   to do or say things which favour sb's progress towards some goal
  different   to **back** implies provide money (financial backing) for a
              particular project
10 similar   literally, both mean to come into flower
   different   figuratively, **bloom** is to reach one's potential, or be
               successful, whereas **blossom** is used more for becoming
               able and confident in one's social activities
11 similar   mental awareness
   different   **conscious** is in a state of having one's faculties working so
               that one is aware of what is around one; **conscientious** is
               having a responsible positive attitude towards one's work
               or the tasks one is supposed to do
12 similar   both refer to other people who share characteristics with
            another and others
   different   **peers** are similarly aged members of the same social
               group; **equals** have the same amount of a given quality

8   complimentary adjectives: sterling, educated, mature, devoted, accurate
    neutral or pejorative adjectives: weird, dull, suspicious, recalcitrant,
    frivolous, dim, coloured
    example collocations: **weird** happening, scene, noise, sight,   **dull** person,
    teacher, play, film   **sterling** type (person), person, character   **suspicious**
    nature, person, noise   **educated** person, voice, manners   **recalcitrant**
    child, student, animal   **mature** person, attitude   **devoted** friend, mother,
    daughter, husband   **frivolous** idea, party, attitude, comment
    dim person, student, child, pupil   **coloured** man, woman, child,
    community   **accurate** assessment, account, statement, bill

9   1 sign up   2 raise   3 hold, earn   4 hooked   5 broaden   6 set
    7 bring   8 show   9 hold   10 launch

10 1 to start doing something the outcome of which is unknown
    2 a on alternate nights   b all other nights   c most nights *coll*
    3 to look forward to something with keen anticipation   4 long narrow
    mark made by some dirt on something   5 to prepare one's bag for a
    journey   6 a club where karate (a form of self-defence) is practised
    7 the thing which is fashionable *coll*   8 a wide range   9 breeding
    from closely related animals   10 to take part in activities when they are
    just beginning which will later become very widespread

11   1 child, dog, plant   2 look, reply, remark   3 colleague, friend, life   4 university, course, movement   5 meeting, glance   6 victory, sorrow, defeat   7 meal, building   8 number, shoe   9 survey, review, report, investigation   10 undertaking, deal, centre, manager

12   1 incredible   2 dropout   3 larder   4 sob   5 disguise   6 chess   7 rush hours   8 wages   9 enroll   10 hustle

13   1 drugs, alcohol, by extension, anything one enjoys, eg watching football   2 one's outlook, one's mind, a road   3 one's ambition, success   4 a course, an investigation, research   5 a person, a book, an article   6 a sweater, socks   7 a list of names, dates, telephone numbers   8 a room, a bed, a meal   9 crops, fruit trees, gardens, lawns   10 a child, a course of action, a candidate for election

14   a   see Student's Book, grid A6, p12
       b   see Student's Book, grid A4, p10
       c   see Student's Book, grid A7, p13

15   1 a science studying the (social, psychological) behaviour of men and animals   2 shaped like the letter T   3 a sample number of cases (people, animals, plants, chemicals) taken from a large number, and not chosen because of any special criteria   4 an IQ which is not low and not high   5 the numerical results of a test   6 an activity in school which is not part of the academic curriculum   7 group of the same age and social standing   8 a completely developed programme   9 not to be successful, not do very well   10 education for people who have finished their normal school training

16   1 to   2 to   3 to   4 in   5 to   6 on   7 in   8 for

17   1 enhanced   2 aggravated   3 consigned   4 launched   5 coached   6 discarded   7 hampered   8 slapped

UNIT 2

1   1 breakthrough   2 trigger   3 euphoria   4 issue   5 stereotype   6 file   7 satellite   8 beam   9 ingredients   10 gatekeeper

2   1 roses, a beard, corn, cabbages   2 songs, music, voices, a play   3 water, seeds, leaves   4 a secret, sb's identity, sb's name, a secret formula   5 funds, a piece of equipment   6 alcohol, smoking   7 a crowd, seeds, papers, petals, leaves   8 records, letters, documents, bills   9 oneself, somebody, sb's interests, a house   10 goods, food   11 the development of sth/sb, sb's/sth's future   12 information, secrets, a project, plan

3   1 a cord made of animal intestine, stretched tightly across a musical instrument, to produce a high-pitched sound when caused to vibrate   2 to control it one has only to push a button   3 the place where documents and records are kept   4 articles made from metal (in computing,

the opposite of soft ware)   5 free time   6 a hall where justice is
administered   7 a silver-coloured sheet on which pictures are shown in
a cinema   8 computer records where data and facts are stored
9 one who directs a school   10 special light beam which can penetrate
solid substances   11 potatoes crushed to a pulp   12 promise solemnly
13 attach a device to permit others' telephone calls to be heard   14 what
cannot be avoided

4   1 enact   2 subscribe   3 take   4 issue   5 gain   6 explore
7 monitor   8 take   9 raise   10 disclose   11 pledge   12 bring

5   1 upbringing, foothold, job   2 support   3 person, train service, car
4 trade, economy, business   5 skills, knowledge, price   6 -minded
7 project, operation   8 person, project, prediction   9 issue,
importance, question, facts   10 step, project, concern
11 choice, use   12 talents, skills, uses, projects

6   1 meaning   ask God or some other supernatural being to punish,
                    injure or destroy a person or thing
        situation   usually the person or thing has done something bad to the
                    person **cursing** and the person cursing feels very angry or upset
    2 meaning   make furious or angry
        situation   usually by putting the **infuriated** person in frustrating
                    circumstances where he cannot accomplish what he wants
    3 meaning   walk wearily or with effort
        situation   one **trudges** during a very long walk — it suggests some
                    unwillingness on the part of the walker — he is not
                    enjoying himself. Trudging is often associated with
                    difficult conditions for walking, eg snow, mud, heat, cold
    4 meaning   *lit* to bear flowers, *fig* to develop fully, realise one's
                    potential
        situation   a person needs to be in a favourable situation in order to
                    blossom, eg for intellectual blossoming, in a stimulating
                    educational environment
    5 meaning   to make alterations to sth written or drawn
        situation   one usually **amends** sth which is a plan for the future, eg
                    an architectural drawing, a parliamentary bill.
                    Amendments are usually intended to be improvements by
                    those who make them
    6 meaning   to hit, usually with the flat of the hand
        situation   a person **smacks** another when he is suddenly angry about
                    sth not very serious. The recipient is often a child who
                    has done sth wrong
    7 meaning   (of a person) with powers of body and mind fully developed
        situation   usually of young persons who appear to have attained
                    adult attitudes to life earlier than usual
    8 meaning   denoting great quantity, or having or affecting many parts
        situation   **multiple** has a rather restricted distribution, and usually
                    refers to parts or qualities which go to make up a whole,
                    eg multiple achievements, multiple talents (of a person),
                    multiple attractions (of, perhaps, a town)

9	meaning	to stop sth or sb which is moving, between its starting point and its arrival at its destination
	situation	the object or person **intercepted** must be in the course of making a journey. But this can be very widely interpreted, eg one can intercept radio messages
10	meaning	money paid in return for work
	situation	a person receiving **wages** is usually employed on a weekly or daily basis. Wages are normally paid in cash, at the end of the week or day. Wages are normally paid for manual, or semi-skilled, work
11	meaning	old torn pieces of cloth, or torn clothes
	situation	1 **rags** are used for cleaning, eg a car, a floor. 2 people dressed in rags are very poor
12	meaning	*fig* fixed mental image of what an object or type of person is usually like
	situation	**stereotype** can only be used of an object or person which is a member of a set or category. When used of persons, it is often pejorative, ie to suggest sb does not have much individuality

7   1 approval   2 inhibition   3 storage   4 reliance   5 defamation
6 privacy   7 maintenance   8 procedure, procession   9 snooper,
snoopery   10 disclosure   11 emission   12 multiplicity   13 diversity

8   1 for   2 at   3 from   4 up   5 for   6 on   7 from   8 to   9 on   10 of

9   1 see Student's Book, grid B6, p 34
2 see Student's Book, grid B10, p 35
3 see Student's Book, grid B9, p 34
4 see Student's Book, grid B11, p 35

10   1 similar   both make defamatory statements about sb
    different   **libel** must be written; **slander** is spoken
2 similar   both make calculations, and reason using input data
    different   **brain** is human; **computer** is electronic
3 similar   made from potatoes
    different   **mashed potatoes** are boiled then crushed to a creamy
        pulp; **chips** are sliced and then fried in oil
4 similar   try to find out what sb else is doing
    different   **spying** is usually a semi-official activity, organised by a
        company, or national government
5 similar   both mean acting contrary to a law, agreement, or convention
    different   differences are collocational
6 similar   have as a cause or starting point
    different   **originate** stresses the starting point, whereas **stem** stresses
        the cause
7 similar   state the opinion that sb else is responsible for some event
        (usu bad)
    different   **accuse** is the general term; **charge** is used only for official
        accusations by the police
8 similar   both concern the use of an object by sb who is not its owner
    different   **borrow** is obtain the use of sth belonging to sb else; **lend**
        is allow sb to use sth belonging to one

9 similar   alter sth, usu a written document, speech, recording of a
            play, lecture, etc
  different **correct** is to change sth which is wrong and make it right;
            amend is change so as to improve
10 similar   take care of young
  different **bring up** is only used for humans and relates to caring for
            them from the moment they are born until they reach adult-
            hood; **breed** is used for causing animals or plants to reproduce
11 similar   no similarities
  different **sensitive** is likely to be affected by things encountered; *fig*
            one's feelings are sensitive to other's actions; *lit* eg certain
            plants are sensitive to changes in atmospheric pressure;
            sensible is having sound judgement, and a calm attitude in
            difficult situations
12 similar   refers to several capabilities in the same individual
  different **many-sided** is for people (ie having many talents); **multi-
            purpose** is for objects (ie which can be used to do
            different things)

11 1 pry 2 divulged 3 disclosed 4 scattered 5 dispersed 6 crucial
     7 versatile 8 multifarious 9 weak 10 feasible

12 1 *f,l* 2 *m,i* 3 *j,o* 4 *k,w,s* 5 *x* 6 *f,h* 7 *y* 8 *a,w* 9 *u,e*
     10 *z* 11 *d,t,r* 12 *b,v*

Revision Exercises

R1 1 peer 2 dropout 3 maze 4 feedback 5 strain 6 fondle
     7 trudge 8 lure

R2 1 a class, a course 2 a lecture, a course, a conference 3 magazine,
     review 4 pardon, forgiveness 5 one's reason 6 water, pesticide
     7 sb's behaviour, opinion, political views, 8 wealth, honours
     9 one's hair 10 money, a debt

R3 1 similar   pass on knowledge to others
        different **teach** is the general term; **instruct** is usually used for
                  practical skills, eg driving
     2 similar   be responsible for the beginning of sth
        different **initiate** is be responsible for the beginning of sth which is
                  continued by others; **instigate** is cause others to begin
                  some process or course of action
     3 similar   both refer to increasing the effect of an action or characteristic
        different **enhance** is used for good things/events, etc; **intensify** is
                  increase in strength, either of bad or good actions
     4 similar   to get something good or useful to oneself from a situation
        different one may **benefit** from sb else's action, whereas **take
                  advantage of** implies positive action by the subject
     5 similar   place obstacles (either literally or figuratively) in the path of
                  something moving
        different **block** results in no forward movement being possible;
                  obstruct is for temporary or partial delay

6 similar   verbal activity
  different   **reel off** is used about someone speaking long lists of
            things without hesitation
7 similar   [+ move ahead or cause to move ahead] [+ in a continuing
            process] [+ usually gradually]
  different   **evolve** suggests taking a long period of time, and implies
            improvement
8 similar   expressing a bad opinion of sth (of a person, or of a remark)
  different   **scathing** suggests not just criticism but an attitude that the
            thing being criticised is so bad as to be hardly worth
            considering at all
9 similar   which can be depended on to do what it is supposed to do
  different   **sterling,** when used of people, suggests a high moral
            standard of integrity

R4   1 with   2 about   3 for   4 over   5 in   6 with   7 of   8 to   9 in
        10 in   11 by   12 with   13 for   14 on   15 in

R5   1 to post   2 work out   3 dim, thick   4 energy, activity   5 chips
        6 postman

R6   1 breakthrough   2 launched   3 crucial   4 strain   5 commit
        6 dour   7 reeled off   8 displaying   9 blatant   10 benefited
        11 enhanced   12 prudent   13 disclosed   14 aggravated   15 took
        advantage of   16 summoned up   17 versatile   18 intercepting
        19 abuse   20 investigate   21 dispelled   22 amend   23 educated
        24 relegated   25 coached   26 heightened   27 evolved   28 impeded
        29 remote   30 feasible   31 entrusted

R7   CROSSWORD

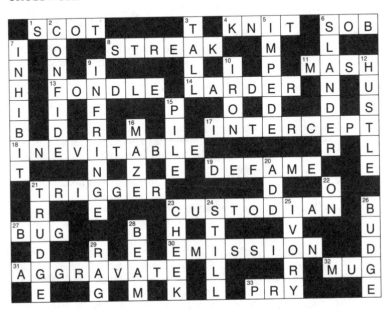

UNIT 3

1 1 barely sufficient budget   2 dishonest person who comes to the door trying to sell something   3 parents and children only living together   4 advice about jobs   5 college for people over sixty   6 areas of a town or city where most people are middle class and move house frequently either for job reasons, or to get a better house   7 groups subsidized by grants from the state or the city   8 length of one's life (in time)/length of a bridge (in space)   9 things in the physical world are constantly changing, disappearing, etc if related to the time-span since the world began   10 prejudice against a person or group of persons on grounds of their sex   11 quick and violent rise of technology due to influence of interdependent factors   12 to shape the history of civilization

2 1 similar   refer to lengths of time
different   an **era** is a period in history, usually dated from some special event, eg the Christian era
2 similar   both dwellings for people
different   a **cottage** is a small house, usually over 50 years old, usually in the country
3 similar   both infringe the law by secretly entering private property
different   the **burglar** definitely intends to steal sth
4 similar   a **thief** is sb who has stolen sth
different   an **alleged thief** is sb who has not yet been proved to be a thief
5 similar   denote the course of time
different   **drag** suggests one feels the time passes slowly because sth boring is happening
6 similar   related to taking property without permission
different   **rob** takes as its object the thing or person from which one takes the property, eg a bank, a householder; **steal** takes as its object the thing stolen
7 similar   related to thinking back to a past event, or past thought or idea
different   **remind** is cause sb to think of sth; **remember** is to think of it oneself
8 similar   refers to lengths of time
different   **eternal** is lasting forever; **temporal** is having an existence measurable in time
9 similar   refer to uneven terrain
different   **mountainous** terrain has many mountains; **hilly** terrain has quite high hills, but not large enough to be called mountains
10 similar   refer to persons having characteristics necessary to participate in some event, course, etc
different   if one is **eligible**, one has the necessary qualifications, nationality, age, etc, but one may not be **fit**, ie healthy enough

3 1 sex, side   2 problems, person, life   3 position, person, group   4 child, person, group   5 parent, aristocrat   6 purpose, task, event   7 patience, variety, possibilities   8 performance, candidate   9 journey, ordeal   10 judgement, person, opinion   11 worker, machine, person   12 illness   13 attendance, companion, temperature   14 mass

4 1 centenarian 2 epidemic 3 soul 4 schedule 5 longevity
6 toast 7 enroll 8 snicker 9 retire 10 overburden 11 solvent

5 1 your promises, your word, the rules 2 risks, expenses, profits
3 your memories, your parents, security 4 your business, your affairs,
a customer 5 a person's character, the course of history 6 sb's attention,
an inheritance, money, a tax rebate 7 a project, a competitor, a race,
a theatrical or musical event 8 air, gas

6 all are partial synonyms or antonyms
   1 syn charming, affecting, sentimental, romantic
     ant dull, repellent, disgusting
   2 syn demanding, exacting
     ant easy, slack, casual
   3 syn delicate, nuanced, slight, gradual
     ant obvious, overt, noticeable
   4 syn far-reaching, large, wide, spacious
     ant small, light, narrow
   5 syn far-away
     ant close by, near, neighbouring
   6 syn old, aged
     ant new, modern
   7 syn enjoyable, stimulating, surprising, unexpected
     ant dull, boring, tedious, straightforward
   8 syn egotistical, selfish
     ant sensitive, considerate, kind, helpful
   9 syn short
     ant long, lengthy, extended
  10 syn saintly, good, moral
     ant wicked, sinful, bad, immoral
  11 syn never ending, endless, infinite
     ant finite, terminable, short-lived, short, fixed-term
  12 syn —
     ant physical, bodily
  13 syn cruel, vicious
     ant gentle, careful, kind
  14 syn special, exceptional, noticeable, significant
     ant ordinary, normal, general
  15 syn complete, total, unmitigated
     ant partial, semi-
  16 syn significant, special, important
     ant minor, unimportant, insignificant

7 1 sponsor 2 persisted 3 shovelled 4 toasted 5 aggravated
6 boisterous 7 thread 8 accomplished

8 1 lady, person, man, woman 2 noise, service, nuisance, interference
3 sky, scene, valley, existence 4 flat, cottage, corner 5 complaining,
noise, questions, problems 6 meeting, decision, doing sth 7 somebody's
arm, a rope, a handle 8 animals, children

9 1 similar continue to exist (for + animates)
different to **survive** is to live longer than, or live beyond an event, often one where one might expect to die, eg an accident
2 similar cause an object to move through the air at speed
different **fling** is throw with great force
3 similar move through, so as to occupy a wide area
different to **pervade** is to spread through, so as to occupy every part of sth
4 similar prove that sth is so
different **confirm** is say that sth suggested, projected or possible, is definitely so; **establish** is state definitely on the basis of evidence
5 similar both relate to being concerned with an event in such a way that one has duties towards it
different a **sponsor** provides money, or a guarantee of money, to allow an individual or group to do sth (eg an academic course, sporting event)
6 similar relate to one's family connections
different **ancestors** are members of one's family from the distant past; **descendants** are members of one's family who follow one
7 similar both describe sections of a complete entity
different a **sample** is a small amount taken from a whole to demonstrate what the whole is like; a **part** can be any size amount taken from the whole
8 similar pass on information about sth bad
different an **admonition** suggests quite formally to sb that they have done sth wrong; a **warning** tells sb that a future event may be dangerous, difficult, or problematic
9 similar both refer to currency used in exchange for goods
different a **subsidy** is a sum of money paid over to enable a non-profit-making enterprise to take place
10 similar concern individual's material wealth
different an **affluent** person is one whose standard of living is above average; a **rich** person has a great deal of money at his personal disposal

10 1 **decline** as a noun has negative connotations when the thing declining is good, advantageous or favoured by the speaker. For example, a decline in moral standards is negative, as is a decline in numbers of people qualifying as doctors, whereas we might say that a decline in the crime rate is positive
2 when a person **begrudges** another's success, his attitude to their success is negative, he is jealous, or feels they do not deserve it
3 **drag on** normally collocates with nouns denoting processes or activities; its implication is always that the thing concerned has lasted for much longer than it should have
4 the object of the verb **overlook** must be sth which in the context should have been done and was not done; overlook suggests human failings like forgetfulness, haste, carelessness
5 **boisterous** is negative when collocating with a noun which the speaker feels should not be boisterous, eg an old lady looking after a child or dog

6 **oblivious** is negative when collocating with a noun denoting sth/sb which should not be oblivious but attentive, watchful, sensitive, etc
7 **incessant** collocates with nouns denoting short, punctual events, and requires a context in which events are repeated many times, and where this repetition is not desired
8 **illiterate** collocates with nouns denoting people who cannot read and write; the implication is usually that the speaker feels that they are deprived
9 **dissonant** collocates with nouns denoting sounds; its use requires that a series of sounds are perceived by the speaker as not harmonious according to the musical sound system he is used to
10 a situation in which **jostling** takes place is usually one where large numbers of people are present and are trying to move quickly in different directions at the same time

11 1 see Student's Book, grid A5, p 51
2 see Student's Book, grid A4, p 51

12 1 heed   2 flung   3 coveted   4 moulded   5 snickered   6 delayed
7 snug, cosy   8 placid   9 serene   10 cared for

Revision Exercises

R1 1 a man-made construction which orbits earth, or another planet, or a planet that moves round a larger planet   2 always according to the same pattern   3 a highly concentrated, single wavelength beam of light, capable of carrying a large amount of energy   4 sudden and important progress   5 to release, to start   6 articles made from metal   7 a servant who opens and closes the gates (to a factory, eg)   8 the parts of a mixture   9 action taken before an event, to prevent possible accidents   10 images from two sources displayed together on the same screen   11 people who analyse material obtained by spying activities   12 to promise solemnly   13 watch constantly, in order to check and quantify the progress of sth

R2 1 see Student's Book, grid B2, p 15
2 see Student's Book, grid B4, p 16
3 see Student's Book, grid A2, p 9
4 see Student's Book, grid A5, p 28
5 see Student's Book, grid A1, p 25
6 see Student's Book, grid A2, p 26
7 see Student's Book, grid A6, p 29
8 see Student's Book, grid B1, p 32
9 see Student's Book, grid B5, p 33
10 see Student's Book, grid B7, p 16
11 see Student's Book, grid B8, p 34
12 see Student's Book, grid A8, p 31
13 see Student's Book, grid B6, p 16
14 see Student's Book, grid A7, p 30

R3   1 to monitor incoming and outgoing telephone calls, usually because of suspicion that the telephone is being used to plan illegal acts, or pass secret information   2 to read the contents without the knowledge of the addressee   3 when one wants to take legal action against sb because they have done one a wrong   4 by accident because one does not realise one is disturbing them, or, in an emergency when one must contact them or when one does not respect their privacy, eg by deliberately listening to a private phone call   5 when there are not sufficient numbers of families for each child to marry sb not from their family   6 when one does not want to be recognized   7 when one acts contrary to the rules or conventions of the club   8 to find sth out about them behind their back

R4   versatile: 1, 3, 5, and 6
sterling: 5, 9, 12

R5   1 see Student's Book, grid A4, p 10
2 see Student's Book, grid A2, p 9

R6   1 *a* [+ make use of to further one's own purposes] *b* [+ do good to]
2 *a* [+ develop intellectual abilities and provide a good cultural background] *b* [+ send to school]
3 *a* [+ pass on knowledge or skill] [+ in certain sports] *b* [+ pass on knowledge or skill] [+ in a particular subject] [+ on a private basis]
4 *a* [+ make worse] *b* [+ irritate]
5 *a* [+ deal a blow] *b* [+ have a strong effect on the mind]
6 *a* [+ be disloyal to] *b* [+ make to be seen what should have been kept secret]
7 *a* [+ act contrary to] *b* [+ disturb] *c* [+ offend]
8 *a* [+ come from or develop from sth else that is the same] *b* [+ obtain (usually a positive feeling or non-material value)]
9 *a* [+ denoting great quantity] *b* [+ having or affecting many parts]

R7   1 desire, want   2 walk   3 hit   4 decline, decrease   5 promise
6 throw   7 obvious   8 important   9 continual   10 emotional
11 optimism, well being   12 push   13 move

R8   1 frantic   2 evolved   3 intercepted   4 breakthrough   5 discovery
6 maintained   7 big   8 large   9 developed

R9   CROSSWORD

UNIT 4

1   1 see Student's Book, grid A6, p 72
2 see Student's Book, grid A3, p 69
3 see Student's Book, grid A2, p 68
4 see Student's Book, grid A5, p 71
5 see Student's Book, grid B6, p 76
6 see Student's Book, grid B7, p 76
7 see Student's Book, grid B5, p 76
8 see Student's Book, grid A2, p 68
9 see Student's Book, grid B4, p 75
10 see Student's Book, grid A7, p 73

2   1 revolting, hideous   2 rude   3 delighted, overjoyed   4 annihilate
5 push   6 scream   7 batter, club

3   1 hoax   2 derail, track   3 plunged   4 mouth   5 subsided
6 guilty   7 character   8 draw   9 from

4   1 in ancient Rome, a man trained to fight at public shows in the arena
2 to make or repair machinery   3 to fit and mend water-pipes,
cisterns, bathrooms, etc   4 to examine newspapers, books, etc, to see
that there is nothing in them that would be offensive or damaging to
potential readers   5 *Am* to care for and heal ill or injured
persons   6 to make or repair electrical machinery   7 to promote the
cause of a pressure group   8 to bring up children

5   1 see Student's Book, grid A7, p 73
     2 see Student's Book, grid B2, p 74
     3 see Student's Book, grid B2, p 76

6   1 similar event or tableau designed for people to look at
      different **display** stresses that the things or people shown are
                 arranged so as to show them off to their best advantage
     2 similar hit sth/sb
      different **batter** is strike repeatedly
     3 similar make holes or incisions in sth with a sharp instrument
      different **hack** is to cut roughly and carelessly
     4 similar (lit) both things you aim at in a game or sport
      different a **goal** is a marked area into which the ball in a team
                 game must pass to score; a **target** is what is aimed at in
                 shooting; figuratively target and goal may be the same if
                 they refer to a general level of achievement; target may
                 also be used for the person or object principally concerned
                 in a scientific experiment
     5 similar used to treat illness or injury
      different **drugs** are usu taken by mouth; **medication** also may be
                 used on the skin for direct treatment to the area of the
                 body affected
     6 similar contain large numbers of books
      different a **library** lends books; a **bookstore** sells them
     7 similar ways of finding out the general conditions of sth (usu large scale)
      different a **survey** can be done of anything; **opinion polls** involve
                 only people, and ask them what they think about sth
     8 similar ways of organising time for a specific purpose
      different **curriculum** refers only to the organisation of lessons in
                 school or other academic courses; **schedule** cannot refer to
                 these but is used for short term events, eg a sale, show,
                 and *Am* train and air timetables
     9 similar people who act dishonestly
      different a **liar** says things which are not true; a **hypocrite** says one
                 thing, and does sth quite different
    10 similar physical damage to the body
      different a **bruise** is a specific kind of injury, consisting of dark
                 marks under the skin, caused by receiving a hard blow
    11 similar well able to express oneself, or well expressed
      different **eloquent** additionally suggests stylistically good speech or
                 writing
    12 similar not saying much
      different one may be **reticent** about one specific topic, but not
                 generally; **reserved** refers to general behaviour as well as
                 speech habits

7   1 society 2 activities, plots 3 attitude, regrets, taste 4 person,
    party, attitude 5 construction, gesture, action, picture 6 behaviour,
    person, act 7 language, behaviour, friend 8 person, house, picture,
    car 9 winner, glance, smile 10 nonsense, hopelessness, futility,
    fabrication 11 face, attitude, appearance 12 wrongs, bodily harm

8 1 someone who has been present at a particular event   2 *Br* not socialist, not conservative; *Am* progressive   3 one who defends civil liberties   4 sexual intercourse outside of marriage   5 the after-effects of drinking too many alcoholic drinks   6 apartment in a building divided into low-quality, cheap apartments, usually in a poor area of a city   7 false bomb alarm   8 nice, admirable, good   9 practical wisdom resulting from experience   10 a set of rails on which trains run   11 inappropriateness (of a situation)   12 the sport of inciting dogs to attack a chained bear   13 language which is not the standard or prestige language used in a given area   14 the act of intentionally taking one's own life   15 honestly   16 strangely enough   17 not to the point, not about the subject under consideration   18 reserved in speaking about sth   19 using bad language   20 holy

9 1 one's passions, anger, temper, desire   2 food, goods, an effect   3 information, false doctrines, ideas   4 one's chances of success, one's reputation   5 one's chances, a friendship   6 one's feelings, creative talent, self-expression   7 problems, answers, solutions   8 books, films, paintings, sb   9 a display, an accident, an event, a crime   10 success, failure, sex   11 traffic, speed, heat   12 feelings, a revolution, a riot, reactions   13 skill, knowledge, ability, goods, products, wares   14 sb from doing sth, oneself, an animal   15 wounds, suffering an unpleasant experience

10 1 see Student's Book, grid A5, p 71
2 see Student's Book, grid A4, p 70

11 1 articulate   2 subdue   3 gratifying   4 battered   5 celebrated
6 propagated   7 fomenting   8 inhibited   9 debased   10 spread

Revision Exercises

R1 1 formal   2 informal, colloquial   3 formal, informal   4 formal, informal   5 colloquial   6 formal   7 colloquial   8 informal
9 informal, colloquial   10 formal   11 formal, informal
12 colloquial   13 informal   14 formal   15 colloquial   16 colloquial
17 informal, colloquial

R2 1 see Student's Book, grid A1, p 7
2 see Student's Book, grid B1, p 15
3 see Student's Book, grid B3, p 16
4 see Student's Book, grid A3, p 9
5 see Student's Book, grid A7, p 13
6 see Student's Book, grid B3, p 33
7 see Student's Book, grid B6, p 34
8 see Student's Book, grid A6, p 12
9 see Student's Book, grid B7, p 34
10 see Student's Book, grid A7, p 30

R3 1 see Student's Book, grid A3, p 27
2 see Student's Book, grid A6, p 52

R4 1 primary school 2 zip, sparkle 3 thick, dim 4 chips 5 postman
6 film 7 boxing 8 pavement 9 to work out 10 enroll

R5 1 see Student's Book, grid A2, p 26
2 see Student's Book, grid B7, p 56
3 see Student's Book, grid B9, p 57

R6 1 eligible 2 substantial 3 boisterous 4 snug 5 esteemed
6 gratified 7 striking 8 aroused 9 placid 10 incited
11 restraining 12 bawl 13 elderly 14 hangover 15 enrolled
16 sponsored 17 banned 18 bluntly 19 eminent 20 outcome
21 subversive 22 propagate 23 stepped in 24 subsided
25 centenarians 26 persisted 27 expedient 28 posed 29 inhibited
30 attacking 31 hoax 32 debasing

UNIT 5

1 1 shell 2 wrinkles 3 slander 4 joke 5 log 6 insult 7 witty
8 campus 9 crevice 10 lottery 11 dialect

2 1 browse 2 stagger 3 cuddled 4 insinuating 5 groan 6 wail
7 blended 8 slide

3 1 a road, the sea when it is calm, a paste which has no lumps in it, a person who is confident and successful 2 someone in a dangerous situation 3 things which can be definitely touched, seen or pointed to 4 things which give a pleasant sensation when touched, eg wool, skin, fur; a soft person is one who gives in to others too easily 5 drugs which are very strong, ie effective 6 people and animals that are quick-witted and scheming for their own advantage are sly 7 of things which are very bad or serious, eg appalling tragedy, accident, appalling exam paper; an appalling person *coll* is one whom you do not like 8 people who inflict suffering on others 9 people who are brave and confident; or, for example, a design which is not intricate or fussy 10 those which are in the process of becoming larger, eg plant, child, new town 11 a message spoken rather than written; someone fluent in the use of language 12 those which one does not like 13 relationships with others, things pertaining to one personally, eg feelings, thoughts, diary, friend

4 *a1:* b6, b7, b10, b15
a2: b2, b3, b11, b16, b18
a3: b1, b2, b3, b4, b6, b7, b9, b11, b12, b13, b15, b16, b17, b18, b19, b20
a4: b2, b3, b4, b12, b13, b16, b18
a5: b3, b6, b8, b12, b19, b20
a6: b6, b12, b14, b15
a7: b5, b12
a8: b1, b2, b3, b4, b6, b10, b12, b14, b16, b17, b18, b19
a9: b3, b18
a10: b3, b6, b12, b1 , b15, b20
a11: b2, b3, b6, b9, b12, b14, b16, b18

a12: b4, b12, b16, b18
a13: b3, b6, b8, b12, b14, b15, b19, b20
a14: b3, b6, b12, b14, b15
a15: b3, b8, b14, b20

5 1 [+ come together] [+ in a group] [+ near each other]
2 [+ use force] [+ make sth move] or [+ move oneself] [+ roughly]
3 [+ read books] [+ without particular goal] [+ usu not reading every page carefully]
4 [+ speak or write] [+ at length] [+ usu without coming to the point]
5 [+ indicate] [+ without saying openly or directly]
6 [+ display] [+ so that others will notice]
7 [+ have as a necessary consequence]
8 [+ change colour of face] [+ red] [+ because embarrassed or angry]
9 [+ continue] [+ to believe in]
10 [+ enter] [+ a place where one is not wanted]
11 [+ have a great affection] [+ such that they cannot act reasonably]
12 [+ practise] [+ a theatrical performance]

6 1 light   2 point   3 shell   4 standing   5 likely   6 fill   7 wear
8 second   9 bear   10 vent

7 1 a target, a goal, a qualification, an arrival time, a group of people
2 TV, films, plays, sports, birds   3 books, magazines, journals, notes
4 feelings, hopes, good relations,   5 mistakes, facts, one's point of view
6 a fire, a cigarette, a lamp   7 a course of action   8 an area of
land, a field for planting, a vegetable patch   9 facts, problems,
opposition, an ordeal   10 a play, an opera, a concert   11 a word, a
telephone number, a reference   12 riches, oneself, a fur coat, diamonds
13 a charge, one's guilt, one's responsibility   14 oneself, one's rights,
a claim   15 old ideas, customs, tradition, one's family, principles

8 1 see Student's Book, grid A8, p 97
2 see Student's Book, grid A6, p 95

9 1 overt, open   2 rough, unsophisticated (people)   3 sly, secretive
4 flexible, floppy, lax   5 modest, humble   6 mental   7 friendly,
cordial   8 friendly, outgoing   9 disappointing, unpromising
10 dried-up, shrivelled   11 nice, kind   12 cold, cold-blooded,
unemotional, ruthless   13 simple   14 unattractive, ugly, nasty
15 practical, realistic, feasible   16 worthless, useless

10 1 see Student's Book, grid A2, p 91
2 see Student's Book, grid A4, p 93
3 similar   related to thinking back to a past event, thought, idea
different   **remind** is cause sb to think of sth; **remember** is to think
of it oneself
4 see Student's Book, grid A9, p 98
5 see Student's Book, grid A5, p 94
6 see Student's Book, grid A1, p 90
7 see Student's Book, grid A7, p 96

8 similar   in both cases attention is focused on a particular object
different   **notice** is to discover for oneself; **point out** is cause sb else
to notice
9 see Student's Book, grid B2, p 100
10 similar   to lead away from right conduct
different   **lure** is tempt (in general with a promise of pleasure);
seduce is more especially persuade a woman to give up her
chastity
11 see Student's Book, grid A1, p 90
12 similar   both refer to knives, forks, spoons, etc
different   **tableware** can be made of any material; **silverware** must be
silver

Revision Exercises

R1   1 make people less good than they were   2 not thinking of sth often
causes accidents   3 used for sth repeated many times so that it is
annoying   4 write bad things about sb which are also untruthful
5 become less effective or less powerful   6 describing sb as smirking
suggests disapproval of their attitude   7 because Christian doctrine says
that desiring to own others' possessions is wrong, English speakers
regard coveting as bad   8 say bad things about sb   9 do some action
against a law or rule, suggests going against accepted moral code
10 again suggests going against accepted code of respect for individual
privacy   11 to tell sth which is not meant to be told   12 a bad
situation becomes worse   13 expressing a negative view of sth
14 sth which deliberately deceives others, goes against accepted code of
honesty

R2   1 sb's reputation   2 water, salt, powder   3 information, a secret, the
real value of sth, sources, plans   4 one's friends, one's country, one's
nervousness, one's real feelings   5 other people's affairs/matters/
business   6 a company, contractor, employer   7 information, goods
8 tea, coffee, fire   9 reactions, riots, protests, demands   10 a letter,
a telegram, a message, a radio signal, a messenger   11 an idea,
possibilities, new territory, unknown lands, outer space, the sea bed
12 smoking (in cinemas), sales of a product, entry, speeding   13 an
agreement, a contract, law, sb's privacy, the charter of human rights
14 sb's office, an embassy   15 people for examinations/for an
athletics contest

R3   1 see Student's Book, grid A3, p 69
2 see Student's Book, grid A1, p 67
3 see Student's Book, grid A4, p 70
4 see Student's Book, grid A6, p 72
5 see Student's Book, grid A5, p 71
6 **suffuse** is spread over the surface of, cover
7 **consent** is be willing to do; to **permit** is to allow to do
8 **relish** is like with excessive satisfaction
9 **filthy** is very dirty
10 **blunt** is rough or plain in speech

11 **witness** is be present and see (so that one can, for example, give evidence in court)
12 see Student's Book, grid A4, p 10
13 **plunge** is thrust forcibly into a liquid
14 **inflict** is cause to suffer

R4   1 see Student's Book, grid A4, p 70
      2 see Student's Book, grid A1, p 67
      3 see Student's Book, grid B4, p 75

R5 A **strike**   [+ deal a blow]
       slap   [+ deal a blow] [+ sharply] [+ using the flat of the hand]
                     [+ sometimes in fun]
       clout   [+ deal a blow] [+ not aiming carefully] [+ hard]
                     [+ especially on the head]
    B **entrust**   [+ hand over or transfer] [+ to the charge of another]
                     [+ based on trust and confidence]
       confide   [+ hand over or transfer] [+ usu private information]
                     [+ often to sb with whom one is on intimate terms]
       consign   [+ hand over or transfer] [+ to the charge of another] or
                     [+ to another place]
    C **educate**   [+ pass on knowledge or skill] [+ develop intellectual
                     abilities and provide a good cultural background] or
                     [+ send to school]
       instruct [+ pass on knowledge or skill] [+ usu in something practical]
       coach   [+ pass on knowledge or skill] [+ in certain sports] or
                     [+ in a particular subject] [+ through extra lessons]
                     [+ often implies the pupil is not up to standard]
       tutor   [+ pass on knowledge or skill] [+ in a particular subject]
                     [+ on a private basis] [+ often implies the pupil is not up
                     to standard]
       train   [+ pass on knowledge or skill]·[+ develop a particular
                     skill or ability by giving practice] [+ in a systematic way]

R6   1 to   2 for   3 round   4 at   5 to   6 after   7 to   8 with   9 from
      10 from   11 to   12 with   13 by

R7   1 beam   2 enacted   3 abuse   4 precautions   5 placid
      6 snickered   7 subversive   8 vernacular   9 reticent   10 sly

R8   1 similar   to make sth known
        different **divulge** suggests the information was not intended to be
                  made known
      2 similar   when used of information, both suggest increasing the
                  certainty of the truth of sth
        different **confirm** is state that sth already suggested is definitely
                  true, whereas **establish** does not imply that the
                  information was already known about
      3 similar   *fig* influencing the way sth or sb develops
        different **mould** can be used for people; **shape** is for abstracts like
                  career, development
      4 similar   not having a particular fact in mind
        different **oblivious** suggests not noticing, not aware, even when the
                  fact is noticeable

5 similar   refer to one's health
  different   **somatic** = physical; **mental** = concerned with the mind
6 similar   both are green and fleshy and grow in the ground
  different   **weeds** are those plants judged not to be useful for food or
  decoration, and therefore not cultivated
7 similar   refer to differences between two things
  different   **disparity** is the difference between two things which are
  similar in other ways; **incongruity** is the quality of being
  inappropriate in a situation because different
8 similar   telling sb that a course of action is not good
  different   **admonition** refers back to a past event; **warning** refers
  forward to an event which has not yet happened
9 similar   money
  different   a **subsidy** is a sum of money given to offset a financial
  loss involved in a project
10 similar   displacing of object from one place to another
  different   **surge** suggests rapid movement of a liquid, eg water, in
  one direction

R9   1 from an association, a meeting, a contract   2 a decision, a meeting,
a trip   3 sb, the passage of legislation, the progress of a meeting
4 a research project, an enquiry, a fund-raising appeal   5 enjoyment,
appreciation, awareness, sensations   6 rules, a contract   7 a fire, a
garden, sheep, pigs   8 person

R10   1 see Student's Book, grid A2, p 26
   2 see Student's Book, grid A3, p 69

R11   1 crowded   2 flock   3 infringing   4 clung   5 dispersed
   6 surprised   7 cared for   8 committed   9 disseminated   10 curd

R12   CROSSWORD

UNIT 6

1 1 palatable   2 inoculation   3 lame   4 labour   5 flabby
6 perfunctory   7 peat   8 scratch

2 1 similar   malfunctioning of the body
different   **diseases** are illnesses passed on from person to person
2 similar   can fly
different   a **jet plane** is propelled by a jet engine; a **propeller plane**
has an internal combustion engine which powers propellers
3 similar   both are responsible for actions of groups of people
different   **foreman** receives instructions from sb more important
4 similar   malfunctioning of the body
different   **infection** is a malfunctioning of part of the body, caused
by (usu temporary) presence of bacteria which the body
cannot fight
5 similar   unpleasant physical sensation
different   **pain** is worse than **discomfort**
6 similar   pass on information to sb
different   **warn** is tell sb in advance of the bad aspects of a future
course of action
7 similar   refer to speeds
different   **brisk** is for speed of running and walking and suggests a
speed which uses a lot of effort for the individual
8 similar   carry blood through the body
different   **arteries** are those blood vessels which carry blood away
from the heart to all parts of the body
9 similar   substances which change the colour of sth
different   **dye** has a permanent result
10 similar   apply pressure to sth to cause to move
different   **yank** is apply sudden, sharp pressure
11 similar   to twist or turn the body
different   **wriggle** can be for a part of the body only; figuratively
wriggle = escape from an undesirable situation, **squirm** =
feel mentally uncomfortable
12 similar   make sth happen
different   **induce** [+ person] suggests persuasion or influence

3 1 one's hands, oneself   2 a cask, sb's chest, a door   3 a cup of
coffee, pudding   4 an orange, your thumb   5 a test, a departure time
6 the truth, an accusation, a signature   7 a mountain, a hill, stairs
8 drinking, smoking, studying   9 one's thumbs, keys, one's hair
10 one's back, one's skin, a car, a floor   11 one's teeth, bones, grain
12 money, treasure, food   13 one's fists

4 1 see Student's Book, grid A5, p 119
2 see Student's Book, grid A3, p 117
3 see Student's Book, grid A6, p 120

5 1 soft, wet earth   2 a town which has mineral springs the water of
which is used as medicine   3 desire strongly   4 offer willingly,
without compulsion   5 a string of beads, twiddled with the fingers to
help ease tension when one is worried   6 a hole with a plug to fit

tightly into it, usu in a bath   7 a drug that causes one to become
tranquil or calm, less nervous   8 ordinary procedure always followed
9 many people having the same disease at the same time and in the
same place   10 continued existence after others of the same kind have
ceased to exist   11 a very small opening in the skin   12 to colour by
dipping in liquid   13 the place where the pilot of a plane sits
14 a medicine that produces a calming effect   15 to clean or wash
with a strong rush of water (eg WC)   16 systematic rubbing of a part
of the body as treatment for pain, discomfort, etc.

6   1 prenatal   2 hoard   3 ingredient   4 yank   5 throb   6 cockpit
7 perfunctory   8 gruelling   9 adamant   10 snarled

7   1 deal successfully with problems   2 over-complicated administrative
organisation   3 one feels bad and responsible because of sth one did
4 different races of man have different physical characteristics
5 decay (of organic matter)   6 grind or crush with the teeth
7 hit hard   8 a special routine for eating   9 long, thin string made of
metal, transmits electric current   10 pull sharply   11 (of human) aggres-
sive way of speaking   12 turn one part of sth, keeping another part still

8   1 inner   2 illness   3 support, side with   4 try   5 curb   6 pull,
jerk   7 fast   8 final   9 adamant, fixed, strong   10 secure
11 harsh, rude   12 dubious, uncertain

9   1 requested   2 pursue   3 marked off   4 lead   5 clasped
6 challenge   7 ran   8 waived

10   1 **dashing**   positive: conveys the idea of boldness, liveliness, and
attractiveness to women
2 **glamorous**   positive: denotes outward charm   negative: implies a
lack of refinement
3 **excessive**   negative: exaggerated
4 **adamant**   positive: firm, determined   negative: inflexible, unyielding
5 **frank**   positive: open, straightforward
6 **gruelling**   negative: exhausting, tiring
7 **clumsy**   negative: awkward, lacking in skill
8 **handsome**   positive: good-looking, attractive
9 **rugged**   positive: (usu of a man) attractive in a strong, masculine
way   negative: (rare), rough, unrefined
10 **firm**   positive: solid, steady, not easily broken, strong, determined
11 **brisk**   positive: quick, active, lively
12 **bright**   positive: cheerful and happy, clever, reflecting or emitting light
13 **harsh**   negative: severe, cruel, rough
14 **slim**   positive: slender, well-formed   negative: insufficient, inadequate
15 **lethargic**   negative: inactive, dull, lacking in energy
16 **morbid**   negative: pessimistic, revealing an unhealthy preoccupation
with death, sickly

11   1 arms, marks, a name   2 suffering, pain, torture   3 jokes, nuts
4 a piece of string, a pencil   5 body, foot, toe   6 monkey, person,
squirrel   7 plant, child, colour   8 mind, plant, part   9 woman,
bushes, chicken

12 1 a division or section of a hospital   2 the office where a doctor gives advice   3 a piece of wood, rubber, metal etc shaped to fit tightly into a hole   4 a bath in mud containing salts (eg as a cure for rheumatism)   5 substances, often in the form of powder, used to flavour food   6 all the set forms connected with a ceremony   7 part of the body where the lungs are situated   8 a long distance race on foot, about 26 miles   9 a place where papers and magazines are for sale   10 *Am* a place where drugs and goods of many different kinds are sold and where ice-cream and fruit drinks are served   11 over-complicated administrative organisation   12 any wearing, monotonous activity

13 1 pressure, speed, temperature   2 work, efforts   3 people who are dissatisfied   4 dreamers   5 people who like keeping things   6 doctors, nurses   7 strength, power, influence   8 plants, wood   9 irritable persons   10 plants, children, investments   11 nervous, restless people   12 dogs, lions, tigers   13 babies, children   14 people who are not concentrating in eg a lecture

14 1 remedy   2 heal   3 bear   4 put up with   5 slender   6 twiddled   7 morbid   8 agile   9 rot   10 constant

Revision Exercises

R1 1 a woman who has lost her husband by death and not married again   2 small folds or ridges on the face   3 a small animal with eight legs that spins a web in which it catches flies   4 the act of alienating or the state of being alienated (estranged)   5 group of people of the same age with whom one is closely associated and similar   6 a native of the West of the USA   7 what can be touched or proved to exist   8 the action of breaking   9 the state of being male, having the characteristics of the male sex   10 loss or impairment of memory   11 the bony framework of the human or animal body   12 a length of wood as it comes from the tree   13 to separate sth into two separate parts (esp of abstract things, eg attitude, situation)

R2 1 up to, up against, under   2 up to, up against, under   3 up to, up (together), under, into   4 up to, up (together), into   5 on, upon, over   6 on, upon, over   7 on, upon   8 across, along, to   9 along, across, over, about   10 from   11 with, into

R3 1 similar   come into a place where one is not wanted
different   **invade** for an army entering another country
2 similar   to read a book, magazine or article
different   **browse** is to read here and there; **peruse** is to read carefully
3 similar   putting two things which were separate together
different   **mingle** [+ the two substances are still separable, identifiable]; **mix** the two substances combine together
4 similar   to make suggestions indirectly
different   **insinuate** is for bad things and suggests that they are not true

    5 similar   high-pitched loud cry

      different **scream** is usually produced with a wide-open mouth and is not used for a sound expressing pleasure; **shriek** may be from excitement or pleasure

    6 similar   walk unsteadily

      different **stumble** is to nearly fall over when walking or running

    7 similar   to move smoothly along

      different **slide** is along a flat smooth surface; **glide** is through air or water

    8 similar   make sth move by applying pressure

      different **to shove** is to push roughly and vigorously, without great care

R4   1 see Student's Book, grid B5, p 76
       2 see Student's Book, grid A5, p 94
       3 see Student's Book, grid B2, p 74
       4 see Student's Book, grid A8, p 97

R5   1 smooth   2 twitches   3 nasty   4 crevice, crack   5 wrinkles
       6 breach   7 rambled   8 gained   9 barred   10 fomented
       11 agonizing   12 placate

R6   1 for   2 in   3 of   4 for, in   5 from, by   6 from, by   7 for   8 from
       9 from, by   10 in   11 from   12 for   13 at   14 at, in, by

R7   1 similar   look on another's advantages with disfavour

      different **covet** is want to acquire another's possessions or position for oneself; **begrudge** is feel another does not deserve what he has

    2 similar   cause an object to move alone through the air

      different **fling** suggests a violent action, not exactly or carefully performed

    3 similar   to cause an event to take place later than planned

      different **postpone** is fix a different definite time; **delay** is cause to be late

    4 similar   *lit* to use a part of the body to attach oneself to sth/sb; *fig* to go on believing in

      different **cling** is hold very hard, with great care, urgency

    5 similar   to obey rules or prearranged agreed procedure

      different **abide by** is more formal

    6 similar   refer to differences between two things

      different **disparity** is the difference between two things which are similar in other ways; **incongruity** is the quality of being inappropriate in a situation because different

    7 similar   money

      different a **subsidy** is a sum of money given to offset a financial loss involved in a project

    8 similar   telling sb a course of action is not good

      different an **admonition** concerns a past event; a **warning** concerns a future one

    9 similar   actions taken relevant to a specific situation

      different **precautions** are actions taken specifically to prepare for something going wrong in the future; **measures** may be the result of past events

10 similar   concerned with the amount of time an event lasts
   different   **brief** is short; **transient** is for sth which stays in one place
              for a limited time
11 similar   *coll* warm and comfortable
   different   **cosy** stresses comfort; **snug** stresses protection
12 similar   associated with calmness
   different   **placid** suggests a nature which is not easily excited; **serene**
              suggests a calm self-confidence

R8   see Student's Book, grid A2, p 68
          see Student's Book, grid A5, p 71

R9   1 perfunctory   2 population   3 exercise   4 appalling   5 huddled
          6 televisions   7 morbid   8 health   9 cure   10 violate   11 palatable
          12 treadmill   13 walk   14 shove   15 crowding   16 insistent
          17 stake out   18 encroached   19 pushy   20 heal   21 infringed
          22 nasty   23 sly   24 tangible   25 breach   26 conceited
          27 remedy   28 yanking   29 postmortems   30 aloof   31 fidgeting
          32 fiddling   33 squirming   34 throbbing   35 flabby   36 wrinkled
          37 sedentary   38 bing-bang

UNIT 7

1   1 become smaller or less powerful   2 to comb or brush one's hair so
         as to give it more bulk   3 express one's disagreement with sb   4 give
         slight or indirect indications   5 eat fast and greedily   6 a society
         where success is the first aim in people's lives   7 ordinary food, not
         specially prepared because there are guests   8 telephone lines for urgent
         messages   9 the ordinary daily tasks in the home   10 set of moral
         principles based on a drive for success   11 time-tables that can be
         modified if circumstances require it   12 periods of work when day is
         divided into several sections covered by different workers

2   1 roar   2 call   3 pamper   4 pass   5 lift   6 try out   7 scrape
         8 mend   9 keep   10 resent   11 reap   12 challenge   13 sack
         14 howl   15 run

3   1 similar   fix the eyes on sth
            different   **glare** is to look fiercely or angrily at sth
         2 similar   periods of the day when there is not much light
            different   **dawn** = beginning; **dusk** = end
         3 see Student's Book, grid A1, p 141
         4 see Student's Book, grid A2, p 142
         5 see Student's Book, grid A3, p 142
         6 see Student's Book, grid A5, p 144
         7 see Student's Book, grid B1, p 148
         8 see Student's Book, grid B2, p 149
         9 see Student's Book, grid A8, p 148
         10 see Student's Book, grid B7, p 150

4 1 one apologizes in a situation where one has done sth wrong, and when one wants to express regret for this 2 if sb succeeds in sth they want to do, one shares their pleasure by offering congratulations 3 when sb says sth bad about one, which is not true 4 when one does not have access to a car, when one has money to pay for it 5 when one wants sb else to do sth 6 usually when one is doing physical work and using up energy, because one is hungry 7 when one has a job and cannot study during the day, usually to learn a new subject or skill 8 at harvest time, to cut corn 9 if one often needs to carry large heavy items over some distance 10 when the grass on the lawn gets too long, one uses a lawn mower to cut it

5 1 see Student's Book, grid A7, p 147
2 see Student's Book, grid B7, p 150

6 1 the floor, potatoes 2 soup, water, vegetables 3 furniture, houses, walls, pictures 4 walls 5 fried food 6 a business, a club 7 goods, relationships 8 paint, paper, mud 9 a car, a truck, a bus 10 a garment 11 paper, hedge 12 one's studies, a point of view 13 evidence, an argument 14 your goals, success, fame, happiness 15 goods 16 a plane, a car, a bicycle, a bus

7 1 devised 2 alimony 3 alibi 4 lumped 5 upbringing 6 dawn 7 gobbled 8 guest 9 hauled 10 harvest 11 rage 12 bloke

8 1 smile, face, expression 2 person, wife, husband, mother, lover 3 remark, letter, person 4 personality, smile 5 meal, dress, pen, person 6 expression, face, nod 7 nurse, doctor, teacher 8 attitude, expression, reception 9 style of dress 10 effect, total 11 person, administration, decision, attitude 12 laugh, meal

9 1 placated 2 muttered 3 mumbled 4 scrubbed 5 dexterity 6 mended 7 solitary 8 expounded 9 despised 10 pampered

10 1 see Student's Book, grid A6, p 146
2 see Student's Book, grid A7, p 147
3 see Student's Book, grid A4, p 143

Revision Exercises

R1 1 invention protected by a patent (= sole right to make or sell sth) 2 a piece of wood in a door, wall, etc, above or below the surrounding woodwork 3 a set of shelves with doors in front of them 4 person who sells medicines or shop which sells medicines 5 a piece of paper, etc fastened to an object and showing what it is, where it is to go to, etc 6 tranquilizer, sedative 7 direct approach, not sensitive to needs of person concerned 8 the ropelike tissue connecting the navel of the foetus with the placenta 9 process of giving birth to a child 10 study to assess the results of sth 11 life spent sitting at a desk, for example 12 a medicine that acts against a poison 13 soft, not firm muscles 14 television 15 medical examination

R2 1 see Student's Book, grid A5, p 94
2 see Student's Book, grid A4, p 93
3 see Student's Book, grid B3, p 100
4 see Student's Book, grid A2, p 91
5 see Student's Book, grid A1, p 90
6 see Student's Book, grid A8, p 97
7 see Student's Book, grid A2, p 116
8 see Student's Book, grid A3, p 117
9 **grind** is rub together harshly with a circular motion so as to produce a dull noise
10 see Student's Book, grid A4, p 118
11 see Student's Book, grid A5, p 119

R3 1 a doctor who specializes in mental diseases and looks after the mentally ill   2 breaks into houses and shops to steal things   3 hears and decides cases in a law court   4 prepares medicines   5 makes things with wood   6 is in charge of a group of workmen in a factory 7 delivers the post   8 maintains and works with technical equipment, often helping others to use it   9 studies astronomy, the science of the sun, moon, stars and planets   10 operates on people   11 keeps a shop 12 flies planes or helicopters   13 is in charge of sth   14 studies plans and builds electrical equipment

R4 1 see Student's Book, grid A4, p 118
2 see Student's Book, grid A3, p 117

R5 1 be shaken (mentally) by hearing sth very special and shocking 2 comfort, freedom from pain, trouble or anxiety   3 a careless mistake 4 shock, astonish sb   5 overwhelm, make sb think a lot   6 pass on, spread from one person to another (of ideas, beliefs, etc)   7 speak in a hesitating way   8 put a large amount/number of things into a small space   9 move or pass gradually into sth, eg dishonesty   10 the action of breaking a law, a promise, etc

R6 1 when one is bored   2 when one is embarrassed   3 when one is angry with sb   4 when one is drunk or tired   5 when sth itches   6 when one is angry or disappointed   7 when one is excited 8 when one feels sb does not deserve sth   9 when one is unhappy and emotionally unbalanced   10 when one is angry   11 when one is shocked or greatly surprised   12 when one feels giddy, or when one is drunk

R7 1 Slang expression, used only between friends, usually not old. Usually suggests the person so described is temporarily very angry or upset about sth. Suggests also that the speaker thinks this reaction is unjustified. (cf unit 6, grid A7)
2 A person described as **scrawny** is old and very thin and not attractive. It can also be used to describe vegetation which is thin and undernourished. (cf unit 6, grid A8)
3 A person described as **sprightly** is usually old but still very energetic and able to move fast. It is a compliment. (cf unit 6, grid A5)
4 The person using the word **morbid** is making a negative judgment — stating that the object so described is death-like or pertaining to death. (cf unit 6, grid A6)

41

5 A **hoax** is a description, but usually with no good reason. It consists of making people think a particular event has happened. It is later proved that it has not. (cf unit 4, grid B1)

6 Sb **goads** sb else when they want them to do sth. They apply any kind of pressure to persuade the person. (cf unit 6, grid B1)

7 People often **doodle** when they are bored, or sometimes when they are speaking but have nothing to do with their hands. (cf unit 6, grid A4)

8 Can only be used between friends to describe a third person who is over-excited and angry about sth. Usually suggests that one thinks this anger unjustified. (cf unit 6, grid A7)

9 *Fig* used of a person who feels very embarrassed and uncomfortable in a situation, because of his own or others' actions. Often this squirming is the result of others' words, eg being blamed for sth. Using **squirm** about sb often expresses satisfaction that person was made to squirm. (cf unit 6, grid B5)

10 Sb **sponsoring** sth must have the money to do so, and must want to spend their money on the project involved. Things sponsored are usually attempts at particular achievements, eg sporting, scientific. (cf unit 3, grid B6)

11 For a person or animal to be described as **placid,** they must be very calm, and not likely to change their emotional state suddenly. (cf unit 3, grid A5)

12 A **sues** B when B has done sth wrong to A, eg not paid him money owing. A will previously have tried to get some recompense and failed. He therefore applies to the law to help him. The court would decide whether A's claim is genuine or not. (cf unit 2, grid A4)

13 **Take legal action** refers to the same action as sue, but the expression is used, usually in writing, as a polite way of threatening to sue. (cf unit 2, grid A4)

14 **Realm** *fig* is used in a small set of fixed expressions, eg realm of possibility, probability, the realms of imagination. (cf unit 3, grid A2)

15 A **inhibits** B if A stops B from doing sth. If B is [+ human], A is either [+ human] or some abstract noun designating social pressure, etc. B may also be [− human] in which case it is usually a chemical or drug, as is A. (cf unit 4, grid A3)

R8 1 see unit 2, grid A3   2 see unit 2, grid A6   3 see unit 2, grid A8
4 see unit 6, grid A6,   5 see unit 2, grid B6   6 see unit 2, grid B11
7 see unit 1, grid A6,   8 see unit 6, grid A3

R9 1 see Student's Book, grid A5, p 94
2 see Student's Book, grid A1, p 67

R10 1 cure   2 nimble   3 adamant   4 slim   5 peers   6 hampered
7 remedied   8 declining   9 spoilt   10 disseminated

R11 [+ hard] : 2, 8, 12   [+ excessively] : 10, 5, 6, 13
[+ violent] : 2, 4, 7, 8, 12, 16

R12 1 morbid   2 acid   3 clasp   4 flabby   5 pores   6 scattered
7 nasty   8 repair   9 gain   10 destructive   11 esteem   12 dull
13 profuse

¹S	²T	U	M	³B	L	E		⁴S	P	⁵I	C	⁶E
	I			A			⁷R			N		N
	M		⁸S	N	I	C	K	E	R		C		T
⁹W	I	T					E			I		I
	D			¹⁰I	N	F	L	I	C	T		E	T
¹¹A				N						E		Y
M		¹²H	I	D	E	O	U	S			¹³C	
N		A		I			¹⁴P		O	
E		M		¹⁵C	U	R	B		E		N	
S		P		T			¹⁶C	R	U	D	E
I		¹⁷D	E	R	A	I	L		V		U
¹⁸A	¹⁹S		R		B			E		C
	U			²⁰L	I	N	E	A	R		T
²¹S	E	D	U	C	E			T		²²S
T				²³S	K	E	L	E	T	O	N
A		²⁴F	I	T		C			D		U
G		O		²⁵C	O	V	E	T		²⁶L	O	G
²⁷G	A	S	P		F				E		G
E		T		²⁸D	²⁹A	F	³⁰T		³¹S	N	A	R	L
R		E			P		A			N		E
	³²R	A	T	E		³³P	E	A	T			

UNIT 8

1   1 vantage point   2 dissidents   3 torch   4 flap   5 cardboard
6 dodge   7 parole   8 asylum   9 data   10 ransom   11 necklace
12 assault

2   1 similar   cause death of
different   **slaughter** is usually for animals
2 similar   temporary blemish or problem with body mechanism
different   a **bruise** is a type of injury where surface of skin becomes
swollen and discoloured, usually as result of a hard blow
3 similar   forms of money
different   **cash** is notes and coins; a **cheque** is a signed
representation of money, usually on a special form
4 similar   both connected with breaking the law
different   **larceny** is a specific type of crime where theft takes place
5 similar   related to holding a person against his or her will as a way
of persuading sb else to do sth
different   a **ransom** is a sum of money asked in return for the
release of a hostage
6 similar   keep away from a physical object, or arrange events so that
one does not do sth
different   **dodge** is move quickly to avoid a moving physical object;
for figurative senses dodge is more colloquial
7 similar   to bring air into the lungs
different   **breathe** is cause air to enter and leave the lungs
rhythmically; **sigh** is breathe once in a noticeable way, to
express emotion
8 similar   take sth which one has no right to
different   **steal** is for objects; **kidnap** is for people
9 similar   say that an action performed by sb has happened
different   **thank** also expresses gratitude that the event has happened
10 similar   place an item in the place where it is usually kept
different   **tuck away** is *coll* and suggests keeping sth safe for a
special reason
11 similar   both relate to stopping sb from doing sth
different   **discourage** is to try to make sb decide not to do sth; **deter**
is cause sb to stop a course of action they are pursuing
12 similar   to prevent a sequence of events happening as planned
different   **interrupt** [+ by temporarily stopping it] [+ unplanned];
disrupt [+ by actions which make event difficult to continue]
[+ unplanned]

3   1 degree, qualification, tendency, work, course, career, mind, question
2 person, situation   3 poison, device, action   4 interval, meeting,
letter, encounter, moment, speech   5 feeling, behaviour, tendency,
opinion   6 behaviour, tendency   7 plan, idea, device, invention
8 traffic, area, house, life-style, mentality   9 feeling, opinion, cold
weather   10 wound, shot, action   11 movement, action   12 weather,
day, situation, mood, area   13 parcel, clothing, suitcase   14 remains,
soul, fear, life   15 idea, change, announcement

4   1 anti-social conduct by young people, often breaking the law
2 a bird that kills and eats small animals or birds   3 a policeman who
is not in uniform   4 the most junior rank of British policeman
5 a person believed, but not proved, to be guilty of an offense
6 a tough person, inclined to be violent, with social problems
7 one who assists people with social problems as part of the welfare
programme of the state   8 inside fabric layer of a coat   9 department
in a store where jewellery (rings, necklace, etc) are displayed and for sale
10 counter where protective clothes to wear in the rain are displayed
11 bag with a double bottom   12 whipping or beating   13 information
directly from the source   14 suit made of tweed and costing 60 pounds
15 quickly put one's foot in the way of sth   16 run away
17 be found guilty of a theft of goods or money over a certain fixed
value (in USA)   18 be clever at stealing small items   19 catch a thief
in a store or shop   20 not at work when one should be there
21 kick with one's boot   22 very fast

5   1 release   2 withdraw   3 hold   4 pick up   5 bend   6 meet
7 cope with   8 destroy   9 scrawl   10 credit   11 take up   12 fire

6   [+ violent] : 1, 2, 3, 7, 8, 15, 16
[+ brutal] : 6, 11

7   1 parole   2 larceny   3 adverse   4 meted out   5 ransom   6 looted,
booty   7 hood   8 scrawled   9 ingenious

8   1 similar   related to sb not being guilty of sth
different   acquit is formally state that sb is not guilty, exonerate is
show that somebody is not guilty (cf unit 8, grid A4)
2 similar   go through another's possessions
different   rifle is for small items in a confined space, ransack is for
a whole building (cf unit 8, grid A3)
3 similar   take sth one has no right to
different   shoplift is to steal from a shop whilst it is open
4 similar   move sth to the inside
different   slip in is put in smoothly and easily
5 similar   kill sb
different   assassinate is murder sb important, usually for political
reasons (cf unit 8, grid A2)
6 similar   capable of killing
different   mortal also means lasting until death
7 similar   person responsible for a misdeed
different   convict has been found guilty in law and is in prison as
punishment
8 similar   for carrying liquids
different   jug has handle and is not airtight; bottle has airtight top
9 similar   sth one does
different   an infraction is a type of action which breaks the law
10 similar   vehicles for transport of less than six people
different   a cab is hired for a short journey within a town
11 similar   garments knitted of wool
different   a cardigan opens at the front

12 similar garment covering lower part of body, each leg being
separately covered
    different **slacks** are comfortable trousers for casual wear

9 1 deterred 2 ravaged 3 deplorable 4 embezzling 5 lethal
6 slumped 7 bulky 8 clung

Revision Exercises

R1 1 at 2 for 3 on 4 to 5 to 6 from 7 to 8 at 9 with
10 up to 11 at 12 of 13 from 14 with 15 at 16 out
17 at 18 of

R2 1 see Student's Book, grid A6, p 72
2 see Student's Book, grid A1, p 90

R3 1 reliance 2 coverage 3 shapely, shapeliness 4 agonize 5 rite
6 pursuit 7 stimulus, stimulant 8 loneliness 9 pretence
10 endearment 11 recognition 12 generosity 13 resentment
14 dexterity 15 intensity 16 accountant

R4 1 grunts 2 sneered 3 solitary 4 deft 5 unwary 6 perennial
7 dexterity 8 scrubbed 9 barred 10 growl

R5 1 a problem, a person, a piece of work 2 an employee, an objection
3 a sound, protest 4 a town for sb, the countryside 5 good
relations, discontent 6 desires, hopes 7 a car, a room
8 a business, a hotel 9 convention, the rules 10 a pie, food, one's
meal 11 sb to do st 12 the way, sb from somewhere 13 food,
beer 14 socks, an iron 15 a hint, standards, an idea, sb from a team

R6 1 see grid A6, p 146 2 see grid A7, p 147 for **scrape**; **scratch** is rub
or scrape, especially with the finger-nails, eg to scratch mosquito bites
3 see grid A3, p 117 4 see grid A4, p 118
5 similar bring sth into contact with sth else
    different **tap** is a brief contact, sometimes hard, eg with a hammer
6 see grid A6, p 146 7 see grid B3, p 125 8 see grid B5, p 125
9 similar fold in the fingers of one hand
    different **clench** is close the fingers hard and nervously
10 see grid A5, p 119 11 see grid A8, p 148 12 see grid A6, p 120
13 similar desiring to succeed
    different **competitive** is desiring to succeed at others' expense, as in
a race 14 see grid A8, p 123

R7 1 proving that one was in some other place when a crime was committed
2 skilled workman who makes objects, eg furniture 3 principles of
morality 4 *coll* for man 5 violent and cruel 6 prevent sb from
doing sth by paying him money 7 accommodation and food
8 furious attack 9 motivated by crude sexual desire 10 making
remarks to sb which one has not the position or state to make 11 ten
pound note 12 remedy for everything 13 an extravagant glorifier of
a group to which he or she belongs, who cannot see outside it
14 sudden fit or attack of a disease or emotion (anger, laughter)
15 the allowance made to a woman by her husband by order of court
for her maintenance

R8   1 see grid A9, p 98
2 see grid A6, p 120

R9   1 to kill pain : stop the pain
to kill time : make time seem to pass
to kill a bill : prevent a bill from going through
to kill a proposal : prevent from being accepted
to kill a person : put an end to his life
2 to pick up information : come across
to pick up a parcel : a) collect a parcel from somewhere b) lift a
parcel in one's hands
to pick up a language : learn without being taught
to pick up a hitch-hiker : give him a lift
to pick up speed : increase one's speed
3 a healthy child : not ill
a healthy appetite : the appetite of a healthy person
a healthy climate : good for health
a healthy way : good, sound, appropriate
4 a hearty meal : solid, abundant
a hearty appetite : good
a hearty welcome : very friendly
a hearty support : complete, sincere
a hearty person : friendly and kind, jolly
5 life-span : duration of life
life-jacket : jacket to save people from drowning
life-boat : boat to save people from drowning
life-insurance : insurance against loss by death
life-expectancy : expected average duration of life
life-guard : person with the duty of saving swimmers from drowning
life-size : having the same size as the person or object represented
life-time : the length of time a person lives
life-cycle : the entire series of processes comprehended in the life of
an organism

R10   1 pampered   2 independent   3 hearty   4 dismal   5 constricting
6 resented   7 viciously   8 picked on   9 swore   10 surly   11 reap
12 sneered   13 challenge   14 laden   15 lumped   16 clashes
17 infractions   18 shoplifting   19 deterred   20 delinquency
21 vandalism   22 smashed   23 slashed   24 convict   25 culprits
26 dodging   27 slump   28 glared   29 wry   30 theft   31 dart out
32 nab   33 snarled   34 blind   35 slipped in   36 cheek to cheek

UNIT 9

1   1 a mixture of eggs and milk, sweetened and flavoured, and baked or
boiled   2 fanatic, person who likes sth very much   3 food of little
nutritive value   4 dish of apples covered with a layer of pastry baked
in the oven   5 label with the price   6 a person who shops in a
supermarket   7 blood vessels that are very hard   8 track of destruction
left by a person, animal, or object   9 conditions that cause sth to
become degenerate, to deteriorate   10 standard of nutrition and
healthy eating-habits   11 a serious dog-fight   12 look tangled or
knotted   13 put at ease   14 stop eating and drinking   15 enjoy oneself

47

2 1 similar start sth
different **onset** means the start of sth bad
2 similar meals
different a **snack** is a light meal taken at any hour of the day;
dinner is the main meal of the day
3 similar produced by cows, drunk by humans
different **cream** is the thick, fatty part of milk
4 similar variety of dog
different a **pedigree dog** is purely bred of one officially recognised
breed of dog; a **mongrel** is a mixture of different breeds
5 similar a substance or liquid moves where it should not be
different **spill** is when the substance falls out of sth; **leak** is usually
for liquids escaping through a hole
6 similar cause a door or lid to be shut
different **bang** is close hard and quickly, producing a loud noise
7 similar pass food through mouth to the stomach
different **gobble** is eat very quickly and greedily
8 similar to go away from some place
different **flee** is to leave quickly to get away from something
9 similar divide sth with a sharp-bladed instrument
different **slice** [+ into flat pieces]
10 similar make into smaller pieces
different **mince** is cause to pass through machine with small holes;
chop is make into small pieces with a sharp knife
11 similar cause to come to pieces
different **burst** is for sth which contains things which come out if it
breaks
12 similar repeatedly stopping and starting again
different **intermittent** of sth which stops then starts again; **recurrent**
of sth which happens at intervals

3 1 to put on a salad to make it taste better 2 to flavour meat when
you eat it 3 to sweeten drinks like tea 4 to preserve foods 5 to
make linen white 6 to cook food 7 to tear vegetables into shreds or
strips 8 to serve food in 9 to deposit waste in

4 1 to **chew over** is to think over very carefully 2 inner emotions can
be said to **gnaw** when they continually bother a person 3 (of
discourse) unpleasant 4 (of a person or his actions) resentful and
unforgiving 5 rude, direct 6 rude, expressing anger 7 *coll* make
humble excuses to sb

5 wood-chip, sugar cube, breadcrumb, cake-crumb, lamb chop, stock cube

6 1 vegetables, paper 2 milk, beer, juice 3 potatoes, apples
4 lettuce, vegetables cooked in water 5 salt, pepper, grated cheese
6 a salad, cold food 7 wood, onions, carrots 8 cake, bread
9 water, vegetables, meat 10 water, vegetables, meat 11 milk and
flour 12 an apple, a carrot 13 gum, meat, a sweet 14 cheese,
breadcrumbs, lemon rind 15 potatoes, cheese 16 meat
17 a drink, a soup 18 potatoes 19 a salad 20 dice

7 1 collapsed 2 hounded 3 opt 4 comment on 5 baffled
6 show 7 oozing 8 -feed, -feed 9 crept 10 caught 11 gobbled
up 12 burst 13 lurked

8

1 weather when it is not cold; taste when it is not strong; comment when it is not as bad as it might be
2 remark when it contains a sexual innuendo; estimate when it is not accurate
3 food when it is not fresh; air when it is not fresh; smell smells of sth not fresh; idea when it is not new
4 taste when it tastes strong and flavoured with spices; dish when it tastes strong and flavoured with spices
5 flavour for a pleasant sharp taste; dish for a pleasant sharp taste
6 taste for unpleasant sharp taste; chocolate not sweet; resentment harsh feelings
7 youth with a well-proportioned figure; chance little chance
8 food simple and nutritious
9 curry burning to taste; sauce burning to taste
10 smell strong and noticeable; aroma strong and noticeable
11 sauce not sweet; dish not sweet; rice flavoured with vegetables
12 taste sharp and sour; apples sharp and sour in taste; wine sharp and sour in taste

9

1 donated 2 adolescence 3 chubby 4 abdomen 5 deficiency 6 minced 7 draining 8 freak 9 licked 10 surplus

10

1 meal, money, room, recompense 2 temperature, output, height, earnings, wage 3 discovery, change, advance 4 reaction, life, scene, meeting, article, letter 5 old gentleman, dog 6 rain, complaints, comments, attempts to do sth 7 fumes, smell 8 gas, fungus, plants, berries 9 taste, smell, sight, person, accident 10 taste, song 11 indigestion, appendicitis 12 house, flat, life, affairs 13 man, dog 14 illness, headaches, problem, expenditure 15 cheeks, child 16 apple, flavour

11

1 see grid B1, p 192 2 see grid B3, p 192 3 see grid A6, p 187
4 see grid A5, p 186 5 see grid A4, p 186 6 see grid A3, p 185
7 see grid A2, p 184 8 see grid A1, p 183 9 see grid A1, p 183
10 see grid A10, p 191 11 see grid A9, p 190 12 see grid A8, p 189

12

see grid A1, p 183

13

1 tossed 2 sprinkle 3 shredded 4 grated 5 sneaked 6 crept
7 banged 8 onset 9 crumbs 10 outcry

Revision Exercises

R1

1 see grid B6, p 150 2 see grid A1, p 141 3 see grid A2, p 142
4 see grid A3, p 143 5 see grid A5, p 144 6 see grid A5, p 144
7 see grid A4, p 143 8 see grid A6, p 146 9 see grid A7, p 147
10 see grid A8, p 148

R2

1 at 2 with 3 from 4 in 5 to 6 at 8 for 9 from 10 out
11 at 12 off 13 at 14 at 15 through 16 from, of 17 from 18 to

R3   1 positive, because it is good for an old person to be energetic and physically able   2 positive, courage is a virtue   3 negative, suggests administration is too complicated, lack of efficiency   4 positive of sth or sb meant to protect, eg boots, legislation; negative of sb who is rough and cruel   5 positive if for sth you want to happen, negative of sth you do not want   6 usually negative, ie capable of doing much damage, but sometimes positive, eg lethal rat-poison, kills rats successfully, or lethal mixture of whisky and gin *coll* makes you drunk very quickly, said by sb who thinks this is good   7 negative, expresses disapproval   8 negative, implies that consistency is good   9 usually positive, of a well-balanced, thoughtful, serious person   10 negative, libel is writing sth bad about sb which is not true   11 negative, foment takes only objects which speaker considers negative, eg revolution, trouble   12 positive, skillful, careful   13 negative, violent and cruel   14 negative, steal money from others through business deals   15 negative, as libel, but for spoken utterance   16 positive, prevailing ethic in English-speaking countries favours not telling others how good one is   17 negative, sb who is guilty of a crime is not well-regarded   18 negative, if you believe in maintaining a correct standard language you describe some words outside the standard as slang   19 negative, if the subversive activity is against you and what you believe in, positive if it is for   20 positive, conforming to religious ideas

R4   1 see grid B1, p 170
          2 see grid A6, p 169

R5   1, 3, 7, 8, 10, 12, 15 : see grid A8, p 123
          4, 6, 11, 14, 17, 21, 22 : see grid A10, p 191
          2, 5, 9, 13, 16, 18, 19, 20 : see grid A7, p 121

R6   1 the common feature is water : **ocean** is the great body of salt water that covers almost three fourths of the earth's surface, = the **sea** as a whole; a **lake** is a large area of water entirely surrounded by land; a **pond** is a small body of water, often artificially made; a **puddle** is a small pool of dirty, muddy water, especially on the road; a **river** is a large stream of water flowing in a natural channel; a **brook** is a small stream; a **trickle** is a flow in drops or in a small stream
          2 all describe human vocal expression : to **roar** is to make a hoarse, loud, deep sound, as in to roar with laughter; to **giggle** is to laugh in a nervous, silly way; to **smile** is to laugh in a gentle, mild, friendly way; to **snicker** or **snigger** is to laugh in a sly, half-ashamed way; to **grin** is to smile broadly and in such a way that the teeth can be seen (to express amusement, contempt or satisfaction)
          3 all are ways of reading written matter : to **browse** is to **skim** through or **read** hastily; to **peruse** is to read through carefully
          4 all describe human vocal expression : to **shout** is to **speak** in a loud voice; to **stutter** is to speak in a hesitating way; to **hem and haw** is to speak in a hesitating, stammering or embarrassed way; to **cry** is to call loudly; to **bawl** is to shout and cry loudly; to **curse** is to swear at, to use bad language against; to **mutter** is to speak in a low, indistinct voice, to murmur, grumble; to **mumble** is to speak indistinctly (as when the lips are almost closed); to **babble** is to make sounds like a baby, to talk foolishly

50

5 all are areas of land: **territory** is an area of land ruled by a government or individual or an area or district in which sb does his work; a **province** is a division of a country; land is the surface of the earth in a given section; a **state** is the area occupied by a body of people organized under one government; a **plot** is a piece of ground; a **site** is a piece of ground suitable for building or where sth has been built; an **area** is an amount of surface; a **zone** is an area (usually belt-like in form) with particular features or for a particular purpose
6 all refer to moving sth using physical force: **shove** is **push** hard, the opposite of **pull**
7 all refer to sth becoming less: to **decrease** or **diminish** or to **dwindle** is to grow less; to **deplete** is to empty; to **shrink** is (to cause) to become smaller
8 all refer to token of value used in exchange for goods or services: **salary** is a regular, monthly payment for a person's services; **wages** is the money paid weekly in cash to manual labourers and domestic servants; **money** comes in the form of **coins** or **banknotes**; **cheques** are orders to pay a certain amount; **deposit slip** is a piece of paper showing the amount of money paid into an account at the bank

R7   1 growled   2 grab   3 opted   4 slid   5 lethal   6 ingenious
       7 deter   8 slumped   9 hissed, slunk   10 speaking

R8   1 see grid B7, p 126   2 see grid A6, p 120   3 see grid B7, p 172
       4 see grid A7, p 121   5 see grid A6, p 120   6 see grid A8, p 123
       7 see grid B6, p 126   8 see grid B4, p 125   9 see grid B1, p 32
       10 see grid B5, p 33   11 see grid A5, p 71   12 see grid B1, p 54

R9   1 see grid A3, p 166   2 see grid A1, p 164

R10   1 shrieking   2 destroyed   3 chew   4 suffered   5 strict   6 refuse
       7 giggle   8 goal   9 lively   10 cut   11 rambles   12 cunning
       3 penalty   14 sound   15 efficient   16 prenatal

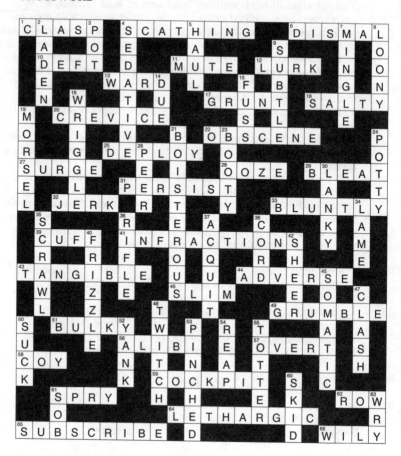

UNIT 10

1   1 locksmith   2 catacombs   3 padlock   4 mole   5 shelter
6 windmill   7 cave   8 courtyard   9 prohibitive   10 residues

2   1 prices that rise very rapidly   2 a place where electricity is generated
3 mechanism which creates artificial heat, mounted on rooftops, using
sun-rays as its source   4 place where a road crosses a railway line
5 4000 square metres of land   6 highways that cross each other several
times   7 buildings constructed on the land surface   8 a machine for
generating or producing power or electricity   9 place where all kinds of
shops are at a walking distance from each other   10 large factory
11 a shop where articles made from metal are for sale   12 road
around a city or town   13 an apartment building in which the units are
owned separately by individuals   14 underground room specially
constructed for storage of valuable items

3 1 allayed 2 issued 3 designed 4 dropped 5 capture
6 overturned 7 stoke up 8 run out 9 broke down 10 rocketed

4 1 light, power, influence 2 offer, deal, contact 3 building, project, construction, edifice 4 buoy, island, oil rig 5 budget, view of the world, account, argument 6 trend, habit, affairs, account, issue 7 monster, site, remains 8 bed, boat, ball, mattress 9 source of energy, energy, resources 10 effect, contact, deal 11 hero, god, journey, battle 12 resources, commodity, food 13 wind, day, draught, room 14 research worker, teacher, nurse, social worker, reformist, supporter

5 1 to power a torch, lights, a radio 2 to carry heavy loads 3 to cool the air 4 to pray to a god 5 to generate energy 6 to warn ships of dangerous places 7 to explore space 8 to drill for oil 9 to melt metal 10 to guide planes or ships, to make planes or ships visible to each other

6 1 similar   area not touched by light
   different   a **shadow** is the dark area formed by the presence of a particular object between the area and the light source; **shade** is the area protected from the heat of the sun by an obstacle
2 similar   bad weather
   different   a **storm** may include rain or snow or hail and must include wind; a **blizzard** is a severe snow storm
3 similar   things which are thrown away or disposed of
   different   **rubbish** is for objects of no use; **waste** is the unused product of a particular process
4 similar   of great value
   different   sth **precious** has universal value; sth **costly** is expensive to purchase because there is demand for it
5 similar   sources of energy which come from fossils
   different   **coal** is a hard stony deposit which can be burned; **gas** is a substance lighter than water, created naturally in pockets under the ground, or artificially by combustion; **oil** is a liquid deposit from underground which can be burned
6 similar   large, important road carrying a lot of traffic
   different   *Br* motorway = *Am* highway
7 similar   consists of animals
   different   **wildlife** is wild animals; **livestock** is animals in captivity, usually for domestic purposes
8 similar   consider sth in one's mind
   different   **ponder** is think carefully and for a long time about sth
9 similar   forms in which water can fall from the sky
   different   **sleet** is half-frozen rain; **snow** is rain frozen into soft particles; **hail** is rain frozen into hard chips of ice
10 similar   have conversation
   different   to **chat** is to speak with sb in a friendly, relaxed way
11 similar   about conveying electric current
   different   **wiring** is a system of wires in a building
12 similar   hard natural substances found in the ground
   different   **fossils** are the remains of once-living plants and animals; a **stone** is solid mineral matter which is not metal

53

7   1 see grid A7, p 211   2 see grid B4, p 213

8   1 a car, a bus, a chair, a theory   2 hay, straw, a house, a city, trees, undergrowth   3 buildings, uneven grounds, roads   4 pain, suffering, poverty, famine   5 pain, suffering   6 animals, records, books, a system, the quality of life, sb's confidence   7 a field, a crop, a house, a pond   8 a village, a town   9 an electrical appliance (hairdryer, television, toaster, radio)   10 a prize, a competition, recognition   11 the lights, the sound   12 fears, doubts   13 evidence, fruit, mushrooms   14 money, valuables, the responsibility for doing sth

9   1 far-fetched   2 faded   3 gloomy   4 blazed   5 fossil   6 chilly   7 residues   8 snag

10   1 see grid A2, p 207   2 see grid A5, p 210
        3 see grid A6, p 210   4 see grid B2, p 213
        5 see grid A6, p 210   6 see grid A6, p 210
        7 see grid A7, p 211   8 see grid A8, p 212
        9 see grid A7, p 211   10 see grid B1, p 213

11   1 alleviate   2 steady   3 demolished   4 allayed   5 razed   6 stout   7 ponder   8 lavish   9 dwindled   10 snag

Revision Exercises

R1   1 the amount of money involved in business operations in a year   2 produce that is (not) treated in a special way   3 eat special foods and avoid others   4 walk along the streets which the policeman has been ordered to watch   5 unexpected return (to public life, for example)   6 show one's teeth in anger   7 more fruit than needed   8 arrange to keep money in a bank in order to draw it out later   9 without having eaten anything for several hours   10 everyone trying to leave at the same time in a disorganized way   11 people eating in a restaurant during the lunch hour   12 a sheet of glass in a motor-car, to protect the driver from the wind (*Br* windscreen)

R2   see grid A4, p 167

R3   1 shock sb deeply   2 change rapidly to a less good condition   3 think over carefully   4 cross out, drop   5 not pleasing to the senses *coll*   6 torment   7 nonsense   8 search through   9 say sth in a rough, unpleasant way   10 find by accident   11 depressing   12 to say forcibly   13 hold in the mind   14 cause to feel ashamed or confused

R4   1 a president, a minister, an ambassador   2 a room, a drawer, an office   3 a plane, a flight, a route   4 classes, negotiations, a service   5 a city, houses, offices   6 the state, a service   7 seals, people, animals   8 a point in an argument, victory, defeat   9 rats, pests   10 a person of sth, a bank, a store, a train   11 pain, the sound of sth   12 money, resources, income, proceeds of an event

R5   1 at   2 on   3 at, on, to   4 away, off, out   5 in   6 over   7 at
8 up, down   9 at, on, to   10 in   11 about, round, around   12 to

R6   1 see grid A3, p 166
2 similar   pass on to sb
   different   **mete out** is only for punishment
3 see grid B1, p 170
4 similar   to take sth which one has no right to
   different   **embezzle** is steal money by manipulating a business in
      which one is involved
5 similar   (of prices) to become lower
   different   when prices **slump** they fall rapidly and far and do not
      rise again
6 see grid A2, p 165
7 similar   prevent sb from doing sth
   different   **dissuade** by telling them reasons why they should not;
      divert by causing them to do sth else
8 similar   covering for the head
   different   **a hood** is attached to a garment; a **cap** is separate
9 similar   person who breaks the law
   different   a **thug** is a criminal who is violent to people
10 similar   period when a convict does not have to be in prison
   different   **probation** is a period of freedom with surveillance by the
      authorities; **parole** is early release in return for good
      behaviour
11 similar   refers to life span of plants
   different   **annual** lasts for one growth season; **perennial** grows for
      several seasons
12 similar   refers to fact of things not being the same
   different   two things are **disparate** when they share some but not all
      characteristics

R7   1 demolition   2 crossing   3 imaginative   4 suspension   5 anxiety
6 greenery   7 fragrance   8 prohibitive   9 deplorable   10 additive
11 deficiency   12 inflatable

R8   1 bulky   2 shredded   3 grated   4 crept   5 crumbs   6 outcry
7 catch   8 comprehend   9 hidden   10 genuine   11 asserted
12 crawling   13 elderly   14 generously   15 precious

R9   1 strike   hit, punch, clout, slap, smack
2 bite   nibble, chew, munch, gnaw
3 kill   murder, assassinate, slay, slaughter, butcher, massacre,
      execute, exterminate
4 talk (informally)   chat, chatter, prattle, babble, blab, gossip
5 soothe/calm   pacify, appease, mollify, placate
6 drink   sip, swill, swig
7 throw   cast, toss, hurl, fling
8 eat   gobble, guzzle, wolf down, devour, gorge
9 fat   obese, corpulent, stout, portly
10 not fat   thin, slim, slender, lean, skinny

R10   1 see grid A10, p 191   2 see grid A9, p 190
3 see grid A8, p 189   4 see grid A6, p 187
5 see grid A5, p 186   6 see grid A3, p 185
7 see grid B2, p 192   8 see grid A1, p 183
9 see grid A1, p 183   10 see grid B1, p 74

R11   1 see grid A6, p 187   2 see grid A4, p 118
3 see grid A2, p 207

R12   [+ violent] : 18, 25, 30
[+ sharply] : 2, 23, 30
[+ excessively] : 4, 5, 7, 10, 21
[+ quick or rapid] : 11, 19, 26, 28, 30

R13   1 packet   2 pavement   3 autumn   4 give up   5 farm   6 engage,
take on   7 biscuit   8 underground   9 petrol   10 car   11 ring road
12 level crossing   13 primary school

R14   2, 3, 6, 8, 9, 12, 14, 15, 18, 20, 21

R15   1 ingredients   2 chop up   3 dice   4 grate   5 finely   6 deficiency
7 licked   8 tossed   9 junk-food   10 freaks   11 gobbled
12 sneaking   13 pinch   14 pie   15 wolf down   16 slip   17 larder
18 crackle   19 detrimental   20 sleet   21 rattled   22 broken down
23 blizzard   24 fragrance   25 filled   26 stoking up   27 roaring
away   28 hardware   29 waste   30 solar energy   31 devise
32 heater   33 flames

R16   CROSSWORD

¹P	L	²U	M	P		³S	N	A	G		⁴D	A	⁵S	H	
O		U				W					E		L		⁶F
N		T		⁷P	I	Q	U	A	N	T		I		L
⁸D	I	C	⁹E	D		G				E		N		A
E			U			¹⁰I			R		K		B
R		¹¹H	C		¹²G	R	A	T	E		¹⁴A	L	L	A	Y
	¹³L	I	C	K		R								
¹⁵F		S		¹⁶C	R	E	E	P						
¹⁷O	N	S	E	T		S		¹⁹G	O	²⁰S	S	I	²¹P
S			A			I				I		E
S		²²T	A	R	T		S		²³I	M	P	E	D	E
I				²⁴I	T	C	²⁵H					L
L		²⁶G		²⁷T		I		U		²⁸G	L	A	R	E
	³⁰D	R	O	O	P		³¹B	A	N	G		U		D
		A		S			L		K		R
³²R	O	B		³³S	L	E	E	T		³⁴C	H	E	W	E	D

56

References and selected further reading

Anthony E M, 'Lexicon and Vocabulary', *RELC Journals* (1975), pp 21-30

Broughton G, 'Native Speaker Insight', *ELT* 32:4 (1978), pp 253-257

Brown Dorothy F, 'Advanced Vocabulary Teaching: The Problem of Collocation' *RELC Journal* 5 (1974), pp 1-11

Channell Joanna M, 'Applying Semantic Theory to Vocabulary Teaching', *ELT Journal* 1 Vol XXXV, No 2 (1981)

Cornu A M, 'The First Step in Vocabulary Teaching', paper presented at the 5th International Congress of Applied Linguistics, Montreal, (1978)

Dagut M, 'Incongruencies in lexical gridding — an application of contrastive semantic analysis to language teaching', *IRAL* (1977), pp 221 ff

Fillmore C J, 'Lexical Entries for Verbs', *Foundations of Language* 4 (1968), pp 373-393
'Topics in Lexical Semantics', in R W Cole, *Current Issues in Linguistic Theory,* Bloomington: Indiana University Press, (1977)

Fromkin Victoria, 'The Non-anomalous nature of anomalous utterances', *Language* 47 (1971), pp 27-52
Speech Errors as Linguistic Evidence. The Hague: Mouton, (1973)

Holec H, *Structures Lexicales et Enseignment du Vocabulaire,* The Hague: Mouton, (1974)

Judd E L, 'Vocabulary Teaching and TESOL: A Need for Reevaluation of Existing Assumptions', *TESOL Quarterly* 12:1 (1978), pp 71-76

Lehrer Adrienne, 'Indeterminacy in semantic description', *Glossa* 4 (1970), pp 87-110
'Static and dynamic elements in semantics', *Papers in Linguistics* 3 (1970), pp 349-374
Semantic Fields and Lexical Structure, Amsterdam: North Holland, (1974)
'Structures of the Lexicon and Transfer of Meaning', *Lingua* 45 (1978), pp 95-123

Luria A R and Vinogradova O S, 'An objective investigation of the dynamics of semantic systems', *British Journal of Psychology* 50 (1959), pp 89-105

Lyons J, *Introduction to Theoretical Linguistics,* London and New York: Cambridge University Press, (1968)

Marshall J C and Newcombe F, 'Syntactic and Semantic Errors in Paralexia', *Neuropsychologia,* 4:2 (1966), pp 169-176

Miller G A, 'A case study in Semantics and Lexical Memory' in A W Melton and E Martin, *Coding Processes in Human Memory,* Washington: Winston, (1972)

Miller G A and Johnson-Laird P N, *Language and Perception,* Čambridge, London and Melbourne: Cambridge University Press, (1976)

Nida E A, *Componential Analysis,* The Hague: Mouton, (1975)

Richards J C, 'The role of vocabulary teaching', *TESOL, Quarterly* 1Q (1976), pp 77-89

Rudzka B and Ostyn P, 'L'Enseignement du Vocabulaire aux Niveaux Intermediaire et Avancé' in J F Matter (ed), *Toegepaste Taalwetenschap in Artikelen* 1, Tilburg, (1976)

van Buren P, 'Semantics and Language Teaching' in J P B Allen and S Pit Corder, *The Edinburgh Course in Applied Linguistics* Vol 2, London: Oxford University Press, (1975)